WAR vs. THE ISLAMIC REBELLION

Thaer Bani Bakr

DEDICATION

First of all, I dedicate this book to my readers and all the truth seekers who take further steps to learn the truth by getting educated and digging for knowledge. Secondly, I dedicate this book to my state, Illinois, and to the most intellectual nation of our current time, the people of the United State of America. I also dedicate this book to my family, especially my grandfather Mousa Bani Bakr, who has been very supportive and helpful throughout the years and decades of my life. And finally, I would like to dedicate this book to one of today's greatest leaders, King Abdullah II of Jordan, who has been a loyal friend and a good ally of our American union.

CONTENTS

WAR vs. THE ISLAMIC REBELLION

AMERICA, THE GREATEST EMPIRE

RECKONING THROUGH MANKIND's PHILOSOPHIES

NAME: 21st CENTURY CIVILIAN

IDENTITY, THE ORIGNIAL FORM & GOD's DILEMMA

NIGHTMARES OF AMERICA

GOD, HERESY, APOSTASY, IDOLATRY IN ARABIA

THE WARNING,

Is a series of seven books, each covering a letter of the word *warning,* as shown on the previous page. In this book, the first letter of the warning is revealed. Thus, this is warning's 1st letter revealed.

The first letter of the warning is about the war against the Islamic rebellion, which is one of the most important topics of the warning. Each letter of the warning series will cover a different subject and will bring light to important issues. The goal is to explain some buried issues that people are trying to understand. The warning is supposed to uncover and allow the reader to discover hidden truths and realities within our world.

War vs. the Islamic rebellion is the first subject of our warning. Even though it's a grim matter, we decided to discuss this material because of the unclear and confusing Islamic terrorism problem that is being conducted by some Muslim imams and their followers. Many of us Americans and Westerners have woken up to find our self, our nation, and our civilization under attack, and most of us don't understand why. Some of us feel that they're attacking our values, some of us think that they hate our religious beliefs, and many of us can see how our foreign policy has increased the global tensions and amount of Islamic terror attacks. The 9/11 attacks were the biggest nightmare of the United States in recent history, and many of us don't know what to say or do to save America and our civilization. Learning and gaining knowledge will help us solve the problem.

Our warning is nothing but a message, and it concerns every conscious, educated and patriotic American. In that sense, *Warning: War vs. the Islamic Rebellion* will enable us to gain a pretty good understanding about why the Islamic terrorists are behaving in such manner and the reasons behind their mysterious jihadi ideology. This warning will allow the reader gain some general insight and awareness about the Islamic rebellion and the war against it.

The rest of the warning series will bring various subjects to the spotlight and will provide more guidance and vision as to what we have in our world. Dear reader, thank you for reviewing the first letter of the warning, which we have offered so you can learn and enjoy the intellectual knowledge that you will gain after reading this book.

A little introduction to this book:

The war has begun, but whether it's a war on terrorism, extremism or Islam, obviously it has been mislabeled. For a better portrayal of this matter, here we provide *Warning: War vs. the Islamic Rebellion,* to explain what has been occurring in the past seven decades. The main problem is that 'if we can't name it, we can't tame it'. Finally, we became aware that the best name for the Islamic jihadism is *Islamic rebelling.* Because not all Islamic terrorists come from jihadi backgrounds, *Islamic rebels* is the most accurate title for such Muslim fighters and militants.

In the year 2008, many of us took to the poles and elected President Barack Hussein Obama to lead us, believing that he would be able to help us eliminate the Islamic terrorism problem and end the Iraq war. Obviously, he did the total opposite; where the Islamic caliphate has been revived and restored under his watch, which his predecessor President George W. Bush has warned of in 2007. For many of us, the 9/11 attacks were the first nightmare; Obama's presidency has become the second one. The Islamic terrorism attacks and Obama's presidency are some of the most worrying and terrifying issues to have ever taken place during the 21st century. Of course, not every American feels that way, but those are the results of the Islamic rebellion and the sequence of the disastrous consequences that the war has brought upon us.

The Islamic rebellion is on the move, and *Warning: War vs. the Islamic rebellion* will detail the evolution of the Islamic rebellious ideology until the reestablishment of the current caliphate; ISIS.

While not all terrorists are jihadists, most jihadists are called and treated as terrorists. President George W. Bush emphasized that jihad is a global threat as it became a terrifying phenomenon, but we can say that the final term for the so-called jihadism is *Islamic rebelling.* Jihadists appear to be criminals, maniacs, radicals, terrorists and, for some, they're holy warriors. But we have come to conclude that jihadists are nothing but religious rebels and political revolutionaries as well. The Islamic rebellion involves large numbers of lost souls and sick individuals who are involved in it. Islamic societies, tribes, or nations are waging jihad today. When young Muslims and excellent students turn from average, civilized citizens into raging killers full of hate of anything that is non-Islamic and fight until death, surely we can recognize that they are extreme religious rebels. In this case, the religion is Islam, so they're Islamic rebels. Today, many casual and random Muslims are rebelling and jihading—although not jihadists. That's the main reason why one must study and learn what's behind their jihad from a rational point of view, so we can deal with the matter accurately and correctly. We must totally understand why the jihadists are carrying on their own wave of apocalyptic and radical agendas. It can be comprehended and completely understood. At the end of the day, they're nothing but men and women, who think, breath, eat and sleep just like us.

In this book, jihadists and Islamic terrorists are redefined as Islamic rebels. The Islamic jihadi campaign is also redefined as the Islamic rebelling movement. According to this standard, *Islamic rebelling* is the new label for the violent jihad. This volume will go further and uncover how the Islamic rebellion has evolved over time. The story goes way back, so this is more like another revelation in the shape of a warning. We will go further and bring some notes into the spotlight which will help us see the bigger picture from a logical point of view. The problem behind this matter is a very long story because of the way it evolved through the past. But we collected all the main points in this guidebook, so you can learn and comprehend every important aspect of it. Examine this apocalyptic literature and take heed; you will not regret what you learn.

The FBI director, James Comey, has stated that some of the things that the Islamic terrorists commit make no sense, even to those who work on such cases for a living. That's the main reason why we have produced this warning, to explain and clarify the Islamic rebellion, which is still on the move until this day. We will detail and point out all that is involved in the evolution of the Islamic rebellion. We'll explain the causes that brought the Islamic rebellious movement this far in its tremendous force and its war versus the Red Nations. We'll lay down the most critical section of the Islamic rebellion; *the Red Nations*, who occupy the most significant part in the current war of the Islamists.

The apocalyptic spirit of the rebellion hasn't died. According to the Islamic apocalyptic doctrine, it's a prophetic rebellion that was initiated by the legendary figure Abraham the Patriarch, remodeled by

Moses the Egyptian, reformed by Muhammad the prophet and recently revived by Bin Laden the jihadist. We'll break down and provide a truthful explanation of the Islamic rebels' jihadism, the reason behind their terrorism and the cause of their rebellion. Frankly, the Islamic political statehood, which Prophet Muhammad formed and called it the caliphate is their ultimate goal.

This apocalyptic literature will describe the Islamic rebellion and how Abraham the Patriarch influenced it. Even though these tales have been taking place for millenniums, the Islamic rebellion could and may come to an end soon. The jihadists believe that the final battle of Armageddon is coming soon, which should be the last jihad to take place before the believers of God are raptured. Today, the apocalyptic events are taking place, whether they're Biblical or Muhammadan events; the Islamic State Caliphate (ISIS) admits it and informs the world that they are conducting the final Holy War. Most likely, within a few decades, this Islamic rebellion can and may end, jihad will stop and finally someone will win, as the Islamic State Caliphate (ISIS) claims. Regardless of what they believe, their jihad and Islamic rebelling could and perhaps will terminate; as the world community along with the cooperation of the Islamic world and peaceful Muslims will bring an end to this conflict. It's like a self-fulfilling prophecy. Concerning the current Islamic rebellion, we may call it the last wave of Islamic jihad and holy wars. We do believe that it will come to an end soon, even though there is a chance that it may last hundreds, if not thousands of years, if left neglected and not treated and cured quickly.

The two main causes that have pushed the Islamic rebellion to its current level of violence are the Jerusalem dispute between the jihadist and Zionist movements and the political bias within the Islamic world, especially Saudi Arabia and its inhumane acts within the Arabian Peninsula. Even though many people think that the Jerusalem conflict is more important and worthy looking at, the latter is the central problem. The Kingdom of Saudi Arabia went from a theocracy to an autocracy to today's prime tyranny of the Islamic world. The one-sided political rule of Saudi Arabia causes the worst destruction and damage to the world's peace, which should've never been ignored after the 9/11 attacks. Instead, the dictatorship monarchy of Saudi Arabia spreads and exports terror and extreme Islamic influences throughout the world without any checking or questioning until this day.

The irony of it is amazing. At the end of the day, the Islamic rebellion speaks for itself. From the days of Abraham the Patriarch, humanity has been wondering about the prophecies of the Israelites. Finally, the Islamic State Caliphate (ISIS) has come to end the tale. The story is almost complete, and here we have this warning about its outcomes. If the Islamists are rebelling, it's because they finally understand the prophetic revelations. Many others don't understand the revelations yet, and so we try to bring some insight about the final stages.

The reason why we say that the matter is finally revealed to the world is because the Islamic rebellion is not about Jerusalem, money, God or land, as we have come to realize. It's about the overall revolutionary movement that is being conducted by the thousands, if not millions, of Muslims around the world. It's an Islamic rebelling movement that was funded and revived by Osama Bin Laden. The current Islamic rebellion has its own ideological agendas, and the evidence is very visible. The Islamic rebellion is a part of what some call apocalyptic Islam. Apocalyptic Islam is not the same as radical Islam, where radical Islam is about spreading Islam by force while apocalyptic Islam is about initiating another phase of prophecies and biblical apocalypses. Even though both apocalyptic and radical Islam are different ideologies of the same religion, they're all a part of one massive movement that was reformed by Prophet Muhammad in the 6th century.

We will not discuss the Quran, Islam or hadith that Muhammad brought forth; instead, we'll maintain the focus on the main reason of this warning, which is to shed some light on what is going on with the Islamic jihadists and why they're pushing for an Islamic rebellion. There is a massive Islamic rebellion that is taking place today, and the goal of this book is to warn about the main reasons behind it, which is why many Muslims join the Islamic rebelling movement and wage jihad. This book is not meant to examine the religious aspect of Islam or the Quran; better yet, it's to confirm that Bin Laden and his Al-Qaeda organization have paved the way for Armageddon, which many call World War III. They claim that they're following the revelations of the ancient prophets and they claim that their actions are biblical and have been mentioned in the Islamic, Christian and Jewish prophecies. We call this book an apocalyptic literature because it provides a rational point of view to the issue but also tries to connect Prophet Muhammad's actions to the current Islamic rebels' wants and desires: which is the reestablishment of the Muhammadan Islamic caliphate.

Ultimately, the main goal of the Islamic rebellion is to make it easier for Islam and Muslims to dominate the world, especially the Holy Lands. The terroristic jihadists are basically sacrificing themselves to assist the Muslim world in gaining control and to produce the next superpower, as they're trying to eliminate the current superpowers: the United States of America and its allies. Obviously, they're moving pretty quickly at their mission as they have accomplished some of their goals already; got rid of some secular Arab regimes and established ISIS.

Our message isn't meant to scare anyone at all. As a matter of a fact, the terror and horrific events have been taking place since Osama Bin Laden formed his Al-Qaeda jihadi group, and since then, the world has witnessed what those sick, mad and violent Muslims have been doing. Our message is meant to bring attention and put the matter in the spotlight and document some of the current events and characters that have been playing a major role in these biblical prophecies. It mostly has to do with our future and warns of World War III. This apocalyptic literature is merely an explanation and another revelation about what is going on with the jihading Muslims and their overall rebellion.

It's all about common sense. Common sense is what we have to rely on to fix these critical matters. As the best of learning animals, we the humans, must keep on with the process of the intellectual struggle against all the difficulties ahead. Watching a drunk driver crash would teach any observer the dangers of driving under the influence of alcohol. Reading this warning and gaining this information on our part is a teaching lesson on the dangers that could accompany the events that are traveling along in our everyday life. We need to keep the learning process going and realize that victory is still possible for the good people of this current civilization.

The jihadism subject is complicated but understandable. The included knowledge is relatively liberating, will free the reader from many misleading information about radical Islam and will also provide straight-forward explanations of the current situation.

We will explain about the head of the Islamic State Caliphate (ISIS) and the people under its authority. This warning is not about frightening any one either. There are many truths in this warning; even if the truth hurts, acceptance must be practiced. Some of the content may seem unbelievable, but that's because of the hidden agendas that the Islamic jihadists carry on behind the public's knowledge.

According to the Muslims, Abraham the Patriarch is the spiritual father of Islam, Christianity, and Judaism. According to Prophet Muhammad, Abraham the Patriarch is the first person who initiated the religious rebelling philosophy approximately 2000 years B.C. Abraham's role is significant to the Islamic rebellion, as he's the man who initiated the monotheist creed and also rebelled against Nimrod, a tyrant of his time. From an Islamic point of view, Abraham's relevant history will be explained from the beginning to the end.

This warning also examines where we stand today, amid the Islamic rebellion and its final war. This book provides a new dimension of understanding to the reader about how Abraham's rebellion came about and relates it to the current Islamic rebellion. It also studies many deals that are taking place currently and compares them to the past.

This book is organized into 10 chapters, called centuries. We have 10 centuries in this book, and each century contains several quatrains. We'll start off with the old stories and realities, and we'll go on and continue until the current caliphate, the Islamic State. Prophet Muhammad's background and actions will also be explained and detailed according to the Muslims view. In the last five centuries, Abu Bakr Al-Baghdadi's character and involvement in the Islamic rebellion will be explained. He's the one who established the Islamic State Caliphate (ISIS) and claims to be from a line of imams that will lead to the hidden Mahdi, an Islamic messianic figure with the end times.

If we're able to get a general understanding of the case in point, then connecting the dots will become easier. Not once have humanity perfected a subject or an object before gaining information, and then learned the elements behind it that gives us a better grip of controlling the matter. By each one of us learning more, then we all can upgrade our agendas and intelligence. That's the most effective way to out power any rivalry and bring a pure-healthy existence back and secure the results.

In order for us to recognize what to do, we need to expand and ensure that we have better information, to connect the dots and make some timeline to create a clearer picture and full comprehension of the reality. This warning makes it real easy to do so by the time the reader is done absorbing the information and will get the bigger picture of the issue in progress. The bigger picture will come to surface, and the reader will gain a better understanding. To display the story in a more intelligible approach, we'll go back in history and start it with Abraham the Patriarch and end it with Ibrahim Awad Al-Badri aka Abu Bakr Al-Baghdadi (Al-Baghdadi II), the founder of the so-called Islamic State Caliphate (ISIS).

We have a little more than 200 quatrains in total among the 10 centuries. Many people have questions about the Islamic jihadism, and we'll go through a lot of them. Answers will be direct and straightforward. We have also placed many curious and controversial questions without answers, which the reader may also find attention-grabbing and will engage the reader in cognitive thinking.

The first five centuries expound the Islamic rebelling's evolution

Centuries 6 – 10 conclude the Islamic rebellion until 2015

Centuries 8 – 10 include the critical and modern information

Quatrains are bold and underlined in this format: **45th and 46th Presidents' duty**

1. Why do today's Muslims rebel and commit jihad?

The jihadism approach

In today's society, some live in gated communities, while others are homeless. In our 21st century, some people still live under cruel monarchs and are still fighting for freedom. Many Muslims oppose such regimes and systems, as most Muslims live in the Old World.

The United States of America gained independence and developed the federal government as a result of the Federalists; the dominant political party back in the late 1700s. But today, 250 years later, the United States of America is a targeted enemy that's at war with the Islamic State Caliphate (ISIS), along more than 50 other jihadi organizations from around the globe. 50+ jihadi groups are at war with America and are included in the advocated 85+ Islamic terrorist jihadi groups that are fighting for an Islamic liberation worldwide. Apparently, most of those Islamic fighters and jihadists are rebelling aggressively for their Islamic freedom every day. Some people may now ask:

Why do some people strive so hard for their cause such as the current Islamic militants? How many jihadists do we have in the world? What's next? Is this a 1000 year conflict and war?

Surely by now, there could be millions of jihadists around the world who are striving for their Islamic liberation and freedom.

Can freedom be achieved?

Dreams can become true. Dr. Martin Luther King had big dreams. Dr. King was dreaming about equality, and the day America had a black president, we realized that everything is possible.

Whether white, black, brown, yellow or whatever others are, we have to keep consideration for all breathing beings. They all should be treated with respect and encouragement, not hate and humiliation. That's why the people of the world look up to America, the mother of the free. Peace, kindness, and gentleness must come with respect for prosperity to be fulfilled. Violence, aggression and madness will bring destruction and cause instability and disorder.

Today

The kick-off at this point of age, in the 2nd millennium is the extreme transgression that we're witnessing. There's a strange and an extraordinary mass transgression that has brought upon us disturbing and curious conditions of total aggression. It seems very devious and evil, and to avoid falling into the error of misjudgment, then one must learn and figure out more about the problem. That's the best way to gain control of the matter that we're facing.

The same way viruses spread around us, and sometimes undetectable for a while, humanity must always detect for risks and possibilities of problems, instead of waiting until it's too late. The world's population has gone from 500 million Muslims in the 1970s to more than 1.7 billion today. The surveys show that up to 20% of Muslims approve jihad and 15% are willing to participate directly in it. Well, the world is scared – better yet, has no clue – what to say to such a mass of people that is angry and on the edge of raising a world war, God forbid. But yes, by now Muslims make up about a quarter of the world's population, and a considerable number of them are involved, partially or directly in this political/religious conflict. At the end of the day, the majority of Muslims are kind and peaceful people. Many of them do seek their freedom, but they want to earn it peacefully and reasonably.

Freedom

Free civilians always control themselves. Patience, joy and goodness can provide positive effects on controlling oneself. Being patient is a necessity in gaining freedom, and it will help keep anger away. The reason the jihadists are angry because they have no freedom.

Free citizens love the mental freedom that they enjoy. Freedom creates an instinct to behave and control oneself. Undoubtedly, if the mental freedom is available, controlling the self and behaving appropriately will become easier to accomplish. Freedom brings peace of mind, which terrorists don't have, and that's why they're out of control.

The United States' freedom of speech laws enables such mental freedoms. The opposite can be seen in the way scholars and thinkers were treated and persecuted in medieval Europe. People fled to America to utilize the peace of mind that America provided for the citizens to enjoy. Millions around the world still dream of reaching this state.

The history of the African Americans demonstrates the importance of becoming free humans. They are a race of constant social struggle, as most of them are still enslaved mentally. The troubling situations in Ferguson, MO, and the riots of Baltimore, MD, over the death of young black males in 2015 affirm the notion that enslavement will fire back; eventually.

Troubled men

Malcolm X, in some sense, was one of the most notable rebels in American history. He chose Islam as his philosophy and died for his belief. By the end of his life, Malcom X was the perfect example of an Islamic rebel, although he did not have the resources and ability to raise a massive Islamic rebellion, as Osama Bin Laden did. It is not just young African Americans suffer from such mental and social enslavement. Today, millions of people around the world feel mentally enslaved, and that can be recognized by looking at the rich people who commit suicides and those who die by overdosing on drugs. They fall in certain situations where they become mentally enslaved.

As correctional and rehabilitation institutions are enslaving wrongdoers by locking them up in penitentiaries, many humans live under major social and mental enslavement, best known as discrimination and favoritism. Discrimination causes mental enslavement, which drives people to even greater sickness. Let's label those victims of the mental enslavement as mentally ill; they're sick people, in other words. The FBI director, Mr. Comey, has addressed this matter before, as he understands the adverse effects of discrimination on society. Today, millions of African Americans have already been imprisoned and became institutionalized and sadly, many of them see the street life as the only way they can live. What's worth mentioning are the enslaved Muslims. Millions of Muslims around the world have been fallen in that enslaved class as well.

Cycles

As old lost souls die, newborn and healthy ones will replace them. If we have sick generations that are unfixable, then we should try to limit the creation of more in the future. That being said, remember that it is a personal responsibility and a social obligation to educate the new ones and teach them what they need to know. New healthy humans should be provided with the best care possible. It is our duty to help the eligible ones so they may avoid enslavement. New humans need to handle their issues to stay mentally free and also manage to become successful and attain their dreams. There won't be total social justice unless opportunities are available for all humans. It doesn't have to be a communist or a socialist system, but equality usually eliminates social problems.

Throughout the Muslim world, millions have been trying to resist inequality within their nations. And by the 20th century, many Muslims went on fighting for their liberty, and some end up rebelling. We'll dig deeper and examine how this issue developed.

The conclusion here is that many people around the world have gone astray from their original state of mind and have been enslaved by the current life system. By now, millions of Muslims have been brainwashed by their leaders, disgusted of their situation and sickened of their history. That's why the angry and sick ones rebel and combat what they see as an enemy that's interfering with their Islamic cause. They rebel and commit jihad to obtain their Islamic freedom and liberation. The Islamic rebellion and liberation cause is about breaking out of the confined limit those enslaved Muslims are experiencing. That's what Bin Laden encouraged the Muslim world do to; gain an Islamic freedom and liberation. He merely revived a new cycle of the Islamic rebellion.

Sick, mad and violent Muslims

Since the establishment of the Jewish Zionist-backed State of Israel in 1948 along the Arab-Israeli war, millions of Muslims have been coming out and calling for war in return. Also, since the collapse of the former Ottoman caliphate in 1924, many Middle Eastern Muslims have been calling and trying to establish a new caliphate. Osama Bin Laden was the founder and leader of the Al-Qaeda organization, which is only one out of the 50+ terroristic jihadi organizations that are waging war on America. The Islamic jihadism and rebellious philosophies of Prophet Muhammad have been their formula of resistance and struggle for their dream: the caliphate. Whether poor and destitute, or rich and wealthy, many Muslims have been enslaved by their horrible past along with the current problems of the Middle East. Many of those who rebel are victims of unjust societies, due to a lack of social justice and widely spread political corruption throughout the Islamic world. They voluntarily rebel and engage in Islamic jihad, following the Muhammadan ideology of Islamic rebelling wars, and jihad.

Why do today's Muslims rebel and commit jihad?

The intensity of current Islamic rebelling movement proves that millions of Muslims are sick of their life. The current turbulent situations of the Middle East have driven many Muslims to rebel, and their rejection of the current worldly system is pretty clear. We will discuss why this enslavement of Muslims became global and fierce, and we'll examine how the Islamic rebellion is changing the world and might change the future of humanity.

So basically, the main reason for today's Muslims to rebel and commit jihad is to gain an Islamic liberation which would allow them to reestablish a Muhammadan caliphate. The caliphate is the Islamic political statehood that was first developed in the 6th century out of the Middle East. By initiating Al-Qaeda, Bin Laden took the first step to combat and remove the regimes of the Middle East, which then would allow the Muslim world to build a united Islamic nation and state.

2. The good, the bad and the ugly realities
The Islamic rebellion's revival

Liberation is the goal of rebellions. The Islamic liberation is what the Islamic rebels, jihadists, and terrorists are aiming for, as Bin Laden explained. In 1988, he and his fellow jihadists formed Al-Qaeda, and that's when they confirmed the revival of the current Islamic rebellion. They took advantage of the injustice that's taking place throughout the Islamic world and reignited the Islamic holy wars.

To decrease our confusion about the jihadism and the terrorism associated with it, we must gain information, identify the issues, keep educated, and stay aware of the issues' components. Knowledge is important in such sensitive subjects and matters.

Truly

Whenever a tornado warning is issued; those who take shelter will be safer than those whom the warning does not reach at all. This warning for the reader is just like a tornado warning, and it is paramount to gain knowledge of the potential threat. We should gain knowledge of all the warnings out there and try to learn of what haven't reached us yet.

What we have out there is a subject in motion and a matter in its evolution. It is very visible physically and understandable mentally. Anyone who is observing the crisis in the world should increase his or her awareness of the matter that's in progress.

Anyone who is aware of the current troubling situations will wonder what the problem is, and this warning will break the matter down to the best explanation possible, directly and frankly. As a part of the effort by our fellow readers, minimal work could be done by opening one's intellectual abilities and using them effectively.

Regarding the Islamic rebellion, we need to look at some principal terms, which we should go through in order for us to get a better idea of the terms. We should take note of the current identification and definition of some of these terms, along with some apparatuses that will help us understand the Islamic rebellion.

Phrases and terms to be familiar with

• **Mankind's struggle** refers to the effort of trying to return to a life of comfort and ease, which is the state of happiness for any human.

The good, the bad and the ugly realities

Food, warmth and shelter are the main struggles of humanity. Mankind must orchestrate their environment to survive with the least destruction and least suffering possible. For thousands of years, humans have struggled to achieve that state. Its mankind's struggle until it's reached.

- **Technology effects** are what make people presume that they control so much. Technology may fool the people, as it can produce an illusion of success. The technology effects of Hitler's campaigns during World War II are a great example, as the invention of the air zeppelins and such technologies, which made him think that he's invincible.

- **Urban vs. rural effects** come when urban areas grow large, as whoever lives in them gets everything delivered to them. Meanwhile, rural effects come in place when people in the rural areas miss the necessities of life. That difference usually raises different wants, needs, and requirements among the people of the two types of societies.

- **Learning vs. brainwashing** are the mental and psychological effects by what people learn and believe versus being indoctrinated and manipulated into believing. Learning involves accepting information. While some people teach truths with common sense, others use lies to deceive and manipulate others. That's what differentiates brainwashing from learning. Learning is rational intellection backed by truths while brainwashing involves deceiving and misleading. Brainwashed people are usually in a hypnotized state of mind, and that's why they usually require a lot of teaching to wake them up from their psychological trip.

- **Population identity** refers to a nation's ethnic identities. For example, the American nation consists of many identities, such as Caucasians, African Americans, Hispanics, and Asians etc. A population can consist of many ethnic groups and religions. The Israeli nation, for example, consists of Jews from all over the world, but not all Jews around the world are Israelis. The same goes with the Islamic world: 15% of Muslims are Arabs, which means that most Muslims are not Arabs.

- **Arabization** is the indoctrination by the Arabs to make them triumph. It's simply a filthy attempt by the Arabs to suck the Muslim world into their den and dominate the world with their culture. Muhammad created Islam, and today's Arabs are trying to connect the Arab world with Islam by spreading the notion of the falsified heritage of Muhammad. Accordingly, Muhammad never differentiated between

The good, the bad and the ugly realities

Arabs and non-Arabs. Arabs today are selling the opposite in order to gain control over the Islamic world. This issue has increased since 1948 after the Arab world was defeated in the war against Israel.

• **The Arabic dream**, which was defined in the year 2000 in a song, is understood as the wish of Arabs to regain control of Palestine and wipe out Israel. It also calls to unite the Arabs of the Middle East and North Africa into one Arabic political state.

• **Islam** is the Muhammadan monotheist philosophy regarding his state and people, who follow the monotheist ideology that was founded by Abraham the Patriarch.

• **Islam's evolution** is the process of the growth of Islam, which began with Prophet Muhammad preaching about Allah and calling to surrender to him. Islam is considered to be a creed and is evolving every day. Islam is the religious base for the spiritual and political philosophy of Muhammad, which has been accompanying humanity for the past 4,000 years; according to Muhammad's account. According to Muhammad, Islam is the creed of Abraham the Patriarch and his God.

• **Islamic liberation,** as we know it today, is the purpose of jihad, where Islamists are trying to liberate the entire Islamic world and unite it under a one central caliphate, as elucidated by Osama Bin Laden. Its main purpose is to regain a worldly Islamic caliphate that would be centralized out of the Mecca and apply an 'Islamic Socialism' model of social justice. The caliphate's main goal is to help Muslims live healthier lives. The 'American dream' for all Muslims is what they're after and is the goal of the Islamic caliphate. The American dream is to enjoy life with a safe environment, get a job, buy a house, buy a car, get married, and have a happy family with a flourishing existence for the children.

• **The caliphate** is the succession of Prophet Muhammad's theological statehood and political arena. It's the political system of the Islamic regime. Muhammad initiated the first Islamic polity in the 6th century out of Saudi Arabia, which became known as the caliphate. The caliphate is where Muhammad applied his Islamic ideology and political philosophy, starting off in Yathrib (Medina) in the Arabian Peninsula.

• **Islamic State Caliphate (ISIS)** is the first caliphate to be established since the abolishment of the Ottoman Empire caliphate in 1924. The Islamic State Caliphate forced its way into existence in 2014, and although it is an illegitimate country according to the U.N., it's a political municipality that evolved out of the Middle Eastern wars and invasions. It evolved from what is formerly known as Islamic State in Iraq and Syria (ISIS), Islamic State of Iraq (ISI), Iraq's jihadi council (MSC), Al-Qaida in Iraq (AQI), and Monotheism and Jihad Group (JTJ). Al-Baghdadi II (shown on the back cover) established it and became the first caliph since 1924. From now on, we'll refer to it as ISC, not ISIS.

   • **Red Nations** refers to the countries and nations that are fighting with the Islamic State Caliphate (ISC), formerly known as ISIS, ISIL, Daesh, etc. The Red Nations is a coalition that was formed by President Obama and was announced in 2014 to combat the caliphate.

   • **Imams** are Islamic preachers and clergies of mosques.

   • **Islamology** refers to the exclusive study of original Islamic jurisprudence. There is the study of Sharia which means the study of Islamic legislation that came out of Muhammad's laws. There is also is the study of Fiqh, which involves the study of Islamic jurisprudence according to Muhammad's style; which some people call Wahhabi teachings or Salafi schools of thought. Within Islamology, we can find the jihad and Islamic rebelling concepts. Any Muslim can study such knowledge, but it does not mean that he's a jihadist. Also, being a jihadist does not mean that the person is an Islamologist. A jihadist could have nothing to do with Islamology and just follow his personal interpretations and enforce jihad by taking actions into his own hands. Every imam, Islamic preacher and cleric is a lecturer of jihad by teaching Islamology; even though he may not be a promoter of violent jihad himself. Warring violently and educating about wars totally differ.

   This book is filled of describing Islamology and will discuss Muhammad's actions and the reasons that allowed the current Islamic rebellion to reach such magnitude of violence and madness.

   • **Jihad** can be described as Islamic rebelling and striving as told by Muhammad's philosophy in Islam. Jihad is an Arabic word that translates to *strive*. Islamists strive for an Islamic liberation, but some rebel in order to retaliate, which consists of war and violent attacks. Jihad might include radical Islamists and sometimes average civilians who also rebel and become jihadists out of nowhere. Some Islamists are neither rebelling nor committing jihad but preach about jihad and

The good, the bad and the ugly realities

Islamic rebelling against oppression. Some men, like Bin Laden, play both roles: Islamist and jihadist.

- **Islamic rebellion** is the social, political and theological movement that developed after the Islamic ideology that Prophet Muhammad formed and applied in the caliphate that he created. During the 6th century's Islamic rebellion, Muhammad applied Hammurabi's code to his social agenda. He introduced Plato's model of social justice in the political arena of the caliphate and used Abraham and Moses's theological prophecies for the religious aspect of the Islamic caliphate.

Why do Islamic rebellions form?

Islamic rebellions have many cycles to form. The cycle starts when social corruption within the Islamic world takes place which brings political corruption, as the people will be misled by the politicians. As social injustice develops, political and diplomatic relations eventually fail. Wars take place and Muslims will be led by the radical imams and Islamologists to wage a sacred duty and strive for the Islamic liberation. Basically, the collapse of the Ottoman Empire caused the Islamic rebellion of the 20th century to develop, and more of its aspects will be described in the next quatrains and centuries.

Global trouble

In today's political arena, each government has the right to armed forces, and governments get to claim territories as their own and enforce their laws. The current caliphate (ISC) is not recognized as a legitimate state by the UN. We'll take a deeper look at it to learn how it developed over the years. The caliphate is what the Islamic rebellion had been calling for, and was reestablished in 2014 out of the Middle East under the black banner of Muhammad's flag of war.

Unfortunately, with all the power and capabilities that current governments have today, there is poverty, oppression, discrimination, favoritism, conflicts, instability and even outrage throughout the world. The Hong Kong protests of 2014 are a result of the unfairness.

Many people around the world are sick of such facts. They know that they're struggling and suffering while a few big shots run the world. The United Nations international agency is the first issue. The UN knows what the problems of the world are and keeps records of the mess. The UN has total knowledge of the progressing mental and physical

The good, the bad and the ugly realities

problems around the world. But since it doesn't do enough, we'll look at some alarming results of its negligence.

But why are the Muslims rebelling so strongly?

By now, we the people realize that there is strife going on around the world between the poor and rich. People wonder why Muslims are the only ones who have the guts to become Islamic rebels and jihadists and pick up arms to terrorize the opposition and try to eliminate oppression. We, the people, have to make note of any infected communities with all cruel systems, since they're the central problem and creator of the Islamic jihadism, terrorism and rebelling that takes place across the world. Let's take Iran, for example. The Iranian people are struggling under the current Iranian tyranny. The Iranians are not Islamists, but they are at risk of rebelling and engaging in jihad against the current hijacked government and autocracy. The people of Iran are living under the Iranian government's repression, and the Iranian people are another great example of Muslims who are potential Islamic jihadists and rebels. Such repression is the main reason for Muslims to rebel.

Viruses can cause illness, but cancerous diseases are much worse and are uncontrollable. We must keep aware of what is going on inside any infected part of the body. Fascism throughout the Islamic world, like Iran, has been like a cancer throughout the Islamic world. The same goes for Saudi Arabia, as the system of inheritance monarchy is against Islamic democracy. Islam's first political state, which became known as the Rashidun caliphate, was based on *Islamic democracy*. The Kingdom of Saudi Arabia is an un-Islamic dictatorship, as the Saudis never get to elect their leaders. Though the Islamic Republic of Iran follows the Islamic democracy model, the brutality and barbarity of the Iranian regime is totally rejected by most of the civilized and educated Iranian people. Both countries, Saudi Arabia and Iran, enjoy peaceful citizens for the most part, but often we see a madman get up, rebel and target those governments with bombs or bullets. They're hijacked nations, per se.

We must follow the rational approach in order to separate truth from fiction and prediction. So we must not pick on the people of a hijacked nation because discrimination is very damaging and there is no room for error while dealing with the crisis that's ravaging the world.

The good, the bad and the ugly realities

Political competition

In general, political rivalries in the world have increased in the past fifty years. Some people are being terrorized at this specific moment somewhere else around the globe. The threat is universal, and in some locations, some individuals could be planning on attacking other right at this moment. Some could even be doing so on our American soil.

What do the civilians need?

Peace: that's what humans need in order to maintain stability. A peaceful environment is required to bring tranquility on mankind. Some people say that there is no peace without war and that war brings peace. Some people want to fight against oppression, they claim.

We should remain aware of the dangers and menaces that might be hunting for us. It is wrong to sit around and just forget about the diseases that could reach us unless one is not worried about his or her health and safety. Evil builds on good people that don't do anything to stop it. We must recognize and realize the role we're involved in as potential victims; otherwise, we could become victims of such awful situations. As Americans, our country is at war, so let's not forget that. We could be attacked at any day without any notification.

Also, we have to keep calm and should not involve our emotions in dealing with such problems. Mental peace within is the most important thing. We need to locate and know where we stand in order for us to keep aggression away. Our safety and personal tranquility are paramount as a civilized nation. We should try to help others to become like us, and maybe as an informed group, we can survive the turbulent events and pass through together as a one solid community. We, as intellectuals, have to take rational consideration of the situation, and hopefully we will avoid getting sucked into the mess, and show others how to avoid the quagmire of instability and insecurity.

Today's leaders

Some leaders seem to add more fuel to the fire. As time passes, we need to understand and try to halt this troubling dilemma of mad leaders who are causing most of the sedition and conflict. Wars aren't the solution, education is. We might have to go out there and give it seventy years, and maybe educate billions of people to fix the problem, but we cannot just give up and let it consume us. It has to be diagnosed as soon as possible; otherwise, those arrogant leaders will keep dragging humanity into worse situations.

Most current leaders care about their legacies more than their nation's wellness.

As long we the civilians do not violate civil and human rights, we could assume that we are fair and just. Sooner or later, those rough rulers and arrogant leaders will find no place to go, and better people will take the lead and replace the corrupted autocrats. Those are the ones that dragged us into the devastation in the first place, and their ignorance of the public's needs is what causes the disasters to increase in size and strength.

Some may say, but most Muslim leaders aren't causing wars at all, so why are their Muslim citizens rebelling and causing the chaos?

The victims of unjust societies

Most Muslims who rebel are mad at their leaders. They feel the injustice within their nations. The same way rebellions occur and revolutions are constantly taking place, we must always realize that correction is their ultimate goal. Rebellions occur when injustice and insufficiency engulf such societies, and no one manages to straighten the wrongs. That's when we must realize that we must manage to balance ourselves and not fall into the same errors as others fell into. People usually rebel for the sake of correcting a problem, and that's why they revolt against those who are causing the problem. Dictatorships and tyrannies always bring problems and cause headaches to humanity and are totally unjust. Look at North Korea for example. The North Koreans are living under one of the cruelest tyrannies that exist today.

We must not let others and their wraths affect us, so we must learn to manage such dilemmas and learn how to stay on the righteous course. We tend to realize that rebellions occur for the simple fact that some people are in need, and that's when rage and madness kick off. We must accept that fact. Hungry stomachs result in theft, depression results in suicides and anger results in homicides.

But some would say, some jihadists are rich and educated, why are they rebelling and committing jihad? Well, that's why we call them sick, mad and violent Muslims; who are enslaved mentally because of their unjust societies and somehow got involved in the Islamic rebellion.

The good, the bad and the ugly realities

For the capable ones

What we're in need of is a solution, and an accurate and complete transformation of this disastrous phenomenon. We shouldn't fight our problems; we must solve them inside out. Every capable person should try to contribute to the solution of our problems. We need to start choosing good leaders and make sure they stay on the righteous course; otherwise we might come face to face with another 9/11, God forbid. We need to advise the children that if they ever become leaders to be good and remind them of the bad ones; hopefully, they will learn from their mistakes. Muslims of America as well should care and help their state and community instead of sitting around and watching the chaos occur.

October 2014…but not just Crimea

As of October 2014, extensive war and chaos have been occurring around the world, as Fox News Channel and CNN showed. Days go by and people forget—because there is newer news every day. By now, most people have forgotten about the problems in Ukraine and Crimea.

Today, many infomercials encourage donations to help our wounded veterans who have lost limbs and for the families of those who lost their lives in the war. What do we gain after getting involved in physical conflicts? It is chaos, and it is very sad when children get hurt. That's where rebellions start: harmed children.

It is our duty as capable and conscious people to stand up and move toward peaceful and reasonable destinations instead of waiting for our ceiling to collapse. A rotten apple infects others, and it could end up infecting the whole farm.

How can we cure humanity if we're fighting a doctrine? How come the Muslims are rebelling using the doctrine of Muhammad? Why did Bin Laden, the Saudi Arabian, choose the philosophy of Islam as his doctrine of war?

The good, the bad and the ugly realities

The nomads and Islam

Osama Bin Laden was born into a bedouin family that comes from the Qahtani tribes of the Arabian Peninsula. Since a young age, his family raised him as a conservative Muslim; one that follows and abides by the Quran and Islamic Sharia law. Not just his family; millions of Arab and bedouin families in the Middle East, North Africa and Central Asia follow the same type of life style. They grow up living a conservative lifestyle by holding an ultra-strict interpretation of Islam.

Islam originated in the desert. From Arabia to West Africa and all the way to China, more than a billion people have taken Islam as the system of operating their daily lives and for administering their lands and civil laws.

Some people wonder why the people of the desert accepted and followed such a system. The answer is: the need. The people of the deserts used to engage in tribal warfare and had such wild lives that they needed some sort of law. Need is what caused the theological system to evolve over the ages. Islam is a system that originated in the desert and that's why most of the desert dwellers of the Old World are Muslims.

When people are in need, they tend to try any method for the sake of their comfort. That's why many Muslims are going back and are trying to refer to Prophet Muhammad's jihadism and rebellious ideologies; they see it as the only way to bring justice back to their societies.

Plus, the indoctrination of the imams and Islamic preachers urges the Muslims to follow Prophet Muhammad's way with dealing with the opposition. By reading and following the instructions of the Quran, they find certain verses and passages they feel will allow them to gain their Islamic liberation. On the top of all that, they think that the Islamic caliphate will help them gain their freedom and will enable them to have better lives by applying the Islamic socialism model of social justice.

3. Ancient legends and rebellious philosophical prophesies
Get to the digging

Let's hit directly at the core and examine what led Prophet Muhammad to initiate the Islamic rebellious ideology. Starting off with the main legend who initiated the monotheist belief system, we'll expound upon how he started it all.

By looking at the Abrahamic creeds, it can be acknowledged that a major figure, more like a founding father, started his program in the Middle East around four thousand years ago as the program is still intact. Abraham the Patriarch, according to Muhammad, played the biggest part for Islam to come about. It's more of a rebellious philosophy than a religion, but later on in time it was transformed into a religious system: prophecy. Let's take a deeper look and examine how and why Abraham did so. We will review his legacy according to the Muhammadan Islamic thought so we can learn why the Muslims and Islamic rebels follow his mentality and way of thinking.

The man known as Abraham the Patriarch has been the hero of the Middle East since his sons had spread throughout the land and brought humanity's attention to them. Avraham is his name in Hebrew, Ibrahim in Arabic, and to us he's known as Abraham. More than half of the world's population believes that Abraham was a Godly man, who had a covenant with the unseen creator of the cosmos. This ideology is very relevant to Muhammad's formation of Islam.

As far as it has been reported, Abraham was a knowledgeable and a genuine man of the Middle East in a part known today as Iraq. But being born far away from his hometown Ur, of southern Iraq, Abraham became used to the wilderness and enjoyed Mother Nature and became a nomad until his return to the city. At that time, there was a brutal ruler of that land known as Nimrod, who was killing newborn boys, for the simple reason that he had a dream that a boy would overthrow him from the throne. That's why Abraham's mother kept him away from Nimrod's jurisdiction, until it was safe for him to return to where they came from.

From natural existence to the city

In order to understand more about the details, we need to take a deeper look at where he was coming from. Abraham was born in the wilderness and grew up in the nature. Once at an older age, he moved back to Ur to find that the town was engulfed with civil disorder, misconduct, and transgression which left him troubled. Slavery, violence, wrath and ignorance were common among the people of Ur at that time.

Abraham grew up as a nomad of the desert. He observed the animals and once he moved to the city, he realized that mankind is in need of a moral revival, otherwise, animals would be more productive and better than humans. Without morals, human civilization can be the worst of the animal kingdom and might develop horrible traits over time. Bad traits such as greed, sloth, gluttony, envy, wrath, pride, and lust are said to grow without a moral system in a society.

The story

Here's how the story seems to go according to Islam. While Abraham was growing up in the wilderness, one day he learned that his father Terah was a minister working for Nimrod. He also learned that the society of Nimrod was corrupted. He observed the actions of the people and recognized that the animals of the wilderness were harmless comparing to the people of Ur as they followed Nimrod's path: the transgression of the wicked and evil man. Abraham was a nomad, so whenever he got hungry, he reached for his sheep and enjoyed its goods, such as milk, yogurt and meat; and he made clothes out of the hair of the sheep. The problem was that Nimrod was celebrated by his people as a mighty man, so they usually obeyed him and submitted to his rule. Nimrod ended up having problems with Abraham every time he complained about the materialism of the people of Ur. People were ignorant, coarse, and violent and also worshiped idols and statues. Abraham complained that the community of Ur was wrongful and going downhill. Abraham understood that he could not be like them and chose to challenge the issue. He went on to explore and find out what was wrong and what wrongs the people made. Even as a teenager, he saw that the people of Ur made no sense; the strong were living off the weak while the weak died off quicker than the strong, just like in the animal kingdom. By his teens, he realized that the people were living in an irreversible madness, which caused him to view them as a sick nation.

As a community, they tended to be stubborn and opposed

Ancient legends and rebellious philosophical prophesies

Abraham's ideas of justice, treating him as if he were an insane person. He concluded that only he could face the reality and change the corruption and wrong habits of Ur. He came to realize that societies are built as a whole and that it's almost impossible to repair them easily. He looked elsewhere to learn other ways of correctness. He had almost no friends aside from his young nephew, Lot, who was more like a brother and a son, and few of the local women who usually had an interest in his ideas and views about life. Abraham had a significant effect on keeping Lot as pure and as honorable as possible. Furthermore, he stayed close to the natural environment and favored the wilderness instead of the city and its inhabitants. In the wilderness, he found more peace and must've felt mad about the wicked authority of the city; Nimrod and his followers. One day, he realized that nature wouldn't let him down, as nature has a perfect sequence of life, day and night, that is unbreakable and a primary source of life. Eventually, Abraham grew out of his fear and came to the conclusion that he needed to do something before his descendants fell into the same misery he found himself in. He always had the gut feeling about a higher power, especially when he examined mankind and their suicidal pride and abuse of power. He eventually concluded that righteousness was the only way to preserve life and that he must be the natural father of his soon-to-come system. Abraham is said to have chased after the system of perfection, as he viewed the natural functioning of life as a consistent, even, and a perfect reality.

Ugly realities

The crooked and bizarre ways people were living was not acceptable by rational people, and Abraham figured that it should be straightened by any means. From that point on, he relied on the forces of nature and his conscious, and decided that he must and should try to defeat such all the evil that he faces. Then he decided to rebel against corruption and its advocates. It is claimed that he preached and argued with his folks, including his father Terah, to the point that his father claimed that he must be a crazy individual.

The rebel out of Babylon

Whether it was natural-born strength or achieved self-built concentration, Abraham was able to overcome fear and rapidly grew brave and encouraged.

Ancient legends and rebellious philosophical prophesies

According to Islam, he chose to attempt miracles by confronting the people, one after another. Once, the residents of his town came to discover that their statue gods had been destroyed except the largest one, and an ax was hung at the statue, dangling from the neck. Abraham was accused of destroying the statues. His response was that "the biggest one destroyed the other ones." They replied that the statues couldn't do such act, and he took advantage of that response and mocked them for worshipping and bowing to idle idols and materials that they imagined as holy deities. His father disowned him. Nimrod had a problem with him, as Abraham challenged him that nature is supreme. They had enough of him and threw him into a fiery furnace, where supposedly, he miraculously neither burned nor died after seven days of continuous fire. Abraham impressed his nephew and some of the women of the area, and seemed like a brilliant man at times. He later migrated to the land of Canaan, Egypt, Palestine and Arabia. His descendants lived on and grew in numbers and still worshiped the creator, God of Abraham. A rebel, a teacher, and a patriarch, that's how he led his troops of sons and descendants. That's where the notion of an active God came from: Abraham and his monotheistic philosophy.

Whether Abraham's actions according to Islam were right or wrong, whether this legend is true or false, and whether he was gifted by God or it's just an ancient myth isn't our concern. His legend that he's a one-man army is what made him a superstar that many men ended up following until this day. His anti-tyranny ideology prevailed, and his system of being a righteous father is still in existence, according to the Muslims. Muhammad claimed that Abraham was the founder of the rebellious ideology and the monotheistic prophecy of Islam.

Common sense

As a man, supposedly, Abraham talked to others concerning daily life issues. As he rebelled against Nimrod, he went on to find good results and a better-straighter path. Abraham began a movement to purify whatever could be purified, and from there he went on to conquer his future. He became a pious man and adapted better virtues. Later on, he had a couple of sons: Ishmael and Isaac. The three built worship sanctuaries all throughout the land to perform meditation and prayers. Even after the death of Abraham, both of his sons kept the faith.

Ancient legends and rebellious philosophical prophesies

His first interest and intention was to obtain and enjoy peace, personally and socially. That's what he wanted: a cultural reform and social prosperity for the average people.

Leaving home and migrating, if necessary

Supposedly, Abraham wandered throughout the lands for more than a hundred years. He saw how miraculous Mother Nature is. During his time, drunkenness in Ur was usual, greed was overwhelming, abuse was widespread, transgression was frequent and humiliation was a regular thing. Social transgressions were constant and unlimited. Social problems were a major issue among the people, as people always relied on the resources of the poor and destitute to accomplish everything, and many weak people were becoming slaves of the wealthy. Abraham sought to eliminate all the evil and mischief from his home, which led the people of Ur to social disasters and malfunction.

Now, compare this detail with Osama Bin Laden, who rebelled and waged war on the government of Saudi Arabia and its allies as he fled the Middle East and went on to Afghanistan to wage jihad. Bin Laden did so in order to escape the Saudi government's prosecution. Prophet Muhahmmad urged on departing from the homeland and committing hijra (migration), as he once also did, copying Abraham in order to get away from the Meccans grip. So basically, there's always a connecting story to the current Islamists following the footsteps of the ancient legendries and the previous rebellious prophets' actions.

A nomad

Abraham opposed all those who blocked him from living a peaceful life, claiming that everyone should seek other solutions for personal liberation, and the sake of his or her family and the community.

To flee Nimrod, Abraham went out and tried other options and roamed in search of better opportunities as he encountered his troubled Babylonian and Mesopotamian homeland. He went mobile with his ideology to try to find a better home and new hope along the journey.

Allegedly, he felt blessed through his travel, as he encountered many communities and cultures, which were flourishing freely at times, although others were doing badly. During his migration, he learned more and appreciated that he'd been given another chance of hope toward the positive and would make the best out of it.

Ancient legends and rebellious philosophical prophesies

Shining for millenniums

The legend claims that Abraham was a brilliant and honorable man with care and compassion for others. His virtue and goodness became the foundation for his monotheistic philosophy. His sons, Ishmael and Isaac, became the first men of Islam and Judaism after Abraham.

It's also claimed that his descendants carried on what he taught about wisdom and about the path of righteousness to avoid wrongdoing so they could succeed as he did. His descendants also moved around and resided all throughout the Middle East as they grew in number and territory. Supposedly, some of his descendants ended up having thousands of descendants. They all adopted his theology and ideology, which Moses used to create Judaism, Jesus used to create Christianity, and Muhammad used to create Islam.

Any order that is connected to Abraham nowadays is considered to include a divine power, which is considered to be faith in God, the supreme power and creator of all beings. In modern days, the Abrahamic creed is separated into cults and sects. Today, Muslims, Jews and Christians make up more than 50 percent of the world's population. They're all followers of Abraham and are believers in his God. According to Abraham, it's an order from God. Abraham created the order to be perfect and walk before the Lord, straight and flawless, as said in the Bible.

Creed or manipulation?

While some people practice religion to find mental relief in it, others use it to create separate cult. While a diverse and a broad span of good and pious principles came along the Abrahamic faiths, some evil men have used religion to justify their cruel rule over the rest.

One good example of such characters is Pope Clement VIII. He brought about many catastrophic events by claiming to be following God's orders. Pope Clement VIII did many horrible things such as persecuting Jews, burning Christian convicts and initiating long wars with Muslims. He used religion to justify his actions and manipulate the masses into doing things that obviously were evil and wrongful.

Ancient legends and rebellious philosophical prophesies

Truth or fiction?

Some people use extreme measures, like brainwashing and psychological indoctrination, by using persuasion, lies and deceit to deceive others into following them; like Hitler did with the young Germans during the 1930s and 40s. This creates confusion throughout the world, as we see young Muslims nowadays making big mistakes by misusing their ancestors' views and inane ideologies to commit terror attacks, which divides the people and creates tensions within mankind.

Religious extremism is just like a tool that some people use to accomplish their goals and desires. The Zionists, the Crusaders and the Islamic jihadists all are perfect examples of men that use the Abrahamic creeds for their gain. While mixing politics with extremism, each of those groups has used its own approach to control certain people and use them as if they are commodities to accomplish political goals.

Relating to Prophet Muhammad

Over a thousand years ago, Prophet Muhammad, the self-proclaimed messenger of God, a descendant of Ishmael, set the policies and laws and established a polity that stood strong for a millennium. Muhammad's philosophy was somewhat similar to that of Jewish and Christian contemporary ideologies. Muhammad's monotheist machine didn't only include physical human resources; it also included the mental power to control his followers. Until Muhammad's empire was worn out due to internal deterioration and political negligence, it was like an American-built muscle car: lubricated and oiled, that lasted for a long time. Muhammad's statehood, the caliphate, collapsed in the early 1900s because of the abuse and lawlessness conducted by the Ottomans.

Since Muhammad was the first leader of his caliphate, which was initiated in the 6th century, there have been various systems and individuals that played role within the Islamic empires and caliphates. The caliphate went on for many generations until the Ottoman Empire, which lasted solidly for about a millennium until it collapsed in 1924.

Purportedly, Prophet Muhammad always introduced voting as a medium for selecting leaders. He learned that political concept from Plato's teachings. Voting, which is integral to democracy, is what Muhammad used to rule his polity. Supposedly, Prophet Muhammad was always voted in by his followers to lead and guide. But eventually, he became an emperor who was elected by his Bedouin people to rule. Although he was a political leader, he was deemed as a religious prophet.

Roman blood vs. human rights

By the 6th century, the Romans had controlled much of the Middle East. At the time Muhammad was alive, the Romans were just a few hundred miles away from him. The Roman Empire considered its people first-class citizens. Muhammad's genius took measures to establish a community that recognized equality and introduced a free civil society. Supposedly, in Muhammad's community, every individual was accepted as a human being with civil rights, regardless of their religious beliefs, ethnicity, class background, gender, age, or skin color. By applying no discrimination between the people, regardless of their tribal powers and strength, his policy was the key to ensure the eternal security of the state by giving no chance for any political rivalries. All were treated the same in his constitution. As described, Muhammad's first constitution was formed by the people of Yathrib (Medina) once he was elected to lead in his new polity in the late 500s. It included civil rights for the Jews, Muslims, Christians, Sabians, idolaters and pagan Arabs in one constitution. It was designed to fill every hole of society; every person had the right to occupy and fill in a particular position.

The constitution of Yathrib established security for the community by barring all weapons within the city, providing religious freedoms, security for women, stable tribal relations, a tax system for supporting the community in times of conflict and parameters for exogenous political alliances. It was a system for granting protection for all individuals and a judicial system for resolving disputes. It also regulated the paying of blood money for murders instead of the revenge killings that were common at the time.

Muhammad drafted the constitution of Yathrib, establishing an alliance among the eight city tribes and Muslim immigrants from Mecca. It specified the rights and duties of all citizens and the relationship of the different communities in the city of Yathrib (known today as Medina), including that of the Muslim community to other communities, specifically the Jews and other "people of the Scriptures" as he named them.

His new law provided general fairness, accepted every law-abiding citizen and established social security and welfare to the unfortunate. The constitution of Yathrib was a general contract derived from a treaty. The deal was built upon the concept of a united community made of diverse tribes living under the constitution.

Roma vs. the Arab

Under the constitution of Yathrib, Muhammad's community united and strengthened its ties. It was the foundation of such policies that encouraged every individual to get involved and join the masses to accomplish his or her duties and responsibilities. That allowed the privileges and benefits of the civil rights that Muhammad placed at the time to form a unity within the city with a solid foundation led by one man.

Usually, any person that speaks in favor of the public's interest will impress, gain support, and lead the masses. Any person with favorable and beneficial ideas will find others paying attention to him/her, standing along with, instead of standing against him/her.

The German self-proclaimed prophet, Adolf Hitler, also made a significant and direct example of such characteristics and ideas for his followers. Hitler's words about the future attracted millions of Germans. Before Muhammad introduced Islam, supposedly, honor killings of young girls by burying them alive in the desert sands were typical. Enslaving the weak and strangers was accepted, and barbaric acts such as material worship and idolatry gave young Muhammad a big advantage in expanding and establishing his own civilized and fair community. Muhammad placed a set of orders and laws that were constituted with a setting of a governing authority with new rules and unique regulations.

Also

Muhammad purportedly collected the best qualities of past regimes and systems and used their experience for his gain. He avoided their mistakes by separating business from family, which allowed him to gain power as he built a united political community. When a few organized individuals establish an organization and recruit talented and skilled individuals, undoubtedly, their state would improve, and bright results would increase within such establishment. Muhammad was an avid follower of Plato's philosophies and political ideas. He implemented Plato's direct democracy in his mosque. Muhammad used Plato's direct democracy model for political resolution and used Hammurabi's code of criminal law to his caliphate. Muhammad used diplomacy to form his structure; which he learned during his youth through the truce negotiations between the Meccan tribes during the tribal wars.

Muhammad and the tribal war

Supposedly, when Muhammad was a young man, a war had been going on between his tribe, Quraysh, against the Qays Alyan tribe. The war continued for many years with a considerable loss of lives on both sides. The war left an bad impression on Muhammad, and he eventually grew brave as he grew older. Quraysh was victorious for the most part, but still, the bloody scenes made Muhammad a sensational individual. Finally, a committee from Quraysh was formed to gain peace and protect the future. Muhammad, who at the time of the event was around the age of 15-17, took a very active role in initiating the peace treaty that came as a result of the settlement of the five tribes involved in the truce. The tribal committee continued to function for a few decades until the introduction of Islam by Muhammad, where he united all the tribes of Arabia into his Islamic caliphate. His involvement in the tribal war enabled him to become a diplomat; to succeed and gain victory.

Diplomacy out of the desert

By bringing a multitude of skills and a diverse array of knowledge together, positive results will eventually come about. That will accumulate achievements more than criminality and malice ever will. A group of church goers will always do better in life and enjoy peace more than a crew of robbers, a barbarian army or even a corrupt state full of betrayals and greedy comrades.

Keep in mind that Muhammad grew up an orphan, but soon enough he became a young shepherd with a few sheep to escort and care for out in the wilderness of the Arabian deserts. Just like Moses the Hebrew, Jethro the Preacher, Abraham the Patriarch, King David of Zion, Jesus Christ the Messiah, and Elijah the Israelite, Muhammad the Bedouin was also a shepherd for some time in his life. Just like the American cowboys of the 1800s, livestock care and animal domestication work has always been prosperous physically and beneficial mentally.

Until his early teens, Muhammad grew up among the Bedouin-Arabs of the Middle Eastern nomads. He then started accompanying his uncle's trade camel-caravans to the northern areas to conduct business in Roman and Persian lands of the Levantine cities such as Jerusalem, Damascus, Palmyra, Baghdad, Anastasia and other populated places of that time. By his mid-twenties, he was leading trade caravans all over the land. Throughout his travel, he learned many things and observed regime systems and learned politics from other civilizations. Political revolutions were the most critical and analytical trend that he mastered through time.

Inspiration

Inspired by Abraham at first, which at Muhammad's time was a 2,500-year-old legend, the Patriarch became the model for Muhammad to follow. Remember that both were nomads who traveled throughout the Middle East and waged those prophetic rebellions.

Muhammad's prophecy

In general, Muhammad was a philosopher, but we consider him the commander in chief of his troops; better yet, he was the emperor of his empire. Muhammad's scripts have been translated into many languages. He shared his knowledge and urged on education. Muhammad's words are a little sophisticated that needs a clear mind to comprehend what he was trying to achieve in his state and mosque. Today, some of his actions may seem to make no sense to many people.

Today, many wonder why many followers of Prophet Muhammad are so brutal. So we ought to take a closer look at some of his extreme followers to try to understand them. But let's keep in mind that some of them are sick in the head and might need some mental help.

Preserving one's life and dying in peace is a lot better than dying violently and wasting life. People should realize that they have the right to enjoy, not just mental peace, but physical peace as well. Let's hope that others can find the means to escape the madness of this world and catch a breath of air and gain peace. We need to look for a way to solve the problems that are facing the future generations. Millions of children around the world are struggling on daily basis, and the world community should find a solution as soon as possible because the UN isn't doing enough. Discrimination is not a healthy thing to do, but one should always recognize what people say and examine their thoughts just to understand their intentions and point of view. One should also check his or her own words and thoughts to evaluate the personal values and standards.

Obviously

It seems that there's a lot that Muhammad did to seize power. His resurrecting of human rights gave him a unique control over the populace and his empire began to grow, even after his death. His philosophy, which he used to form a political statehood, became the machine and the crushing power of Islam. It created the Islamic caliphates and empires, which one-fourth of the global population today is a remnant of.

From all over the world

According to today's Muslims, Muhammad was one of the first barrier breakers when it came to favoritism and discrimination. He evidently preferred certain individuals over others, but he looked beyond age, race and class when he did so. He made friendships with Persians, Romans, Ethiopians and even Asians, and their class and age did not interfere with him recognizing them as the same type of beings. Humans are conscious and have feelings and experience emotions and sense their surroundings. It means that all people deserve fairness and should enjoy privileges as all others do. We must gather information from anywhere, whether it comes from a Muslim or a Jew, White or Black, man or woman, young or old, rich or poor. We could check the authenticity of the information and determine whether to consider them or not. But meanwhile, information should be accepted and recognized, recorded and documented at least for examination and review if not to be followed and applied. Other than the personal performance, all humans are the same and should be treated equally.

Still trying

Fourteen hundred years ago, Muhammad established his polity and governed it for a while, and since then, humanity came to meet the many successors of his empire. But still, since then, we came to know many cruel monarchies, fallacious governments, unjust rulers, and vicious tyrants, regardless of how hard revolutionaries tried to beat such evil by fighting their oppression.

We, as civilians, are still struggling with confusing leaders, deceitful liars, bloodthirsty autocrats, dictators and political criminals.

Ancient legends and rebellious philosophical prophesies

Unfortunately, we're still suffering from the results of such governmental setbacks. Until, we the people eliminate such wrongful men and women, obliterate such systems, abolish injustice, and exterminate favoritism from our world; corruption, bias, and oppression will always find its way into every society.

As prejudice and greed continue, crooks will infiltrate our society and stay subjugating the civilizations. In the next century, we'll go back and take a deeper look at how Muhammad's philosophy became the crushing force that is in operation today, which is called Islam.

Everyone is special somehow

Every person in this world is unique. We must recognize and respect all humans as we do ourselves. We also have the responsibility to teach and educate others as much as possible. Otherwise, equality will remain elusive and divisions will arise. That's how societies split up and fall apart.

Any division and sedition in a community will give other nations the chance to thrive and flourish, and thus other communities will rise while the other is falling behind, and the cycle will go on. After World War II, the United States did not flourish only because of the crushing military force, but because of the good diplomatic relations.

Disastrous

Let's mention some recent problems of our era. Though technology keeps upgrading, more people are depressed and seeking a way out of the daily struggle; in a world where the rich enjoy driving Ferraris and wearing pearl necklaces. There are billions of successful and educated people but still, aggression is expanding, suicides are on the rise, major conflicts are taking place, poverty is increasing, diseases and health concerns are rising, just as the rate of unemployment is growing. We also have water crisis, food crisis, drug abuse, political and social instability, etc. in many parts of the world. Some wonder why we have a bunch of crooked men leading us who leave such problems behind and focus on gaining comfort for themselves while their nations are screwed.

By looking at Chicago, IL, Queens, NY, and Los Angeles, CA, we see many cities suffering from street gangs and criminal enterprises. The mischief and abuse that is taking place is very disturbing. The unfortunate victims cry, but no one helps as they hope.

Ancient legends and rebellious philosophical prophesies

That's all there is to it when solving problems: contain the matter, then try to purify those bad elements out of the troubled situations and individuals. In colleges and universities, professors try to teach about the lack of social justice and blame it on the founding fathers instead of blaming it on the current corrupted leaders and rulers. In some parts of the world, disagreeing with, criticizing or denouncing a leader is punishable by law. In the United States of America, capitalism is supreme, as some people are only worried about the next car, latest movie and newest smartphone. Many Americans are generous and are virtuous people, but the younger generations are growing up very selfish, and many of them think only of themselves.

Solving the issue

We, as a civilized nation, should learn and study all tragic events from around the world, but we should not live in fear. We must remain calm regardless of how desperate the issues get, as some mad men become outraged and take their anger out on others. Troubles should be studied one at a time, even if the individuals need to be examined for mental disturbances. Let's hope all agree that we should concentrate on the children and fix their problems rationally and efficiently. The recent mass shootings occur because of mad individuals, and sure as heaven, that madness has increased since the flower power era. For better results regarding the anger and madness problems, self-control and self-discipline should be taught conclusively at younger ages.

The federal government has been indicating a possible 2nd great depression, so we have to realize that we're facing a serious matter. The reality behind the fact is terrifying and is as dangerous as a heart attack. Some Americans are terrified of Russia, rare Ebola and Islamic terrorists more than necessary. Some claim that it's all a part of a conspiracy to keep us, the civilians, under control.

If we wish to get things fixed, we need to start off with the authority and the political class. But that's one example of how some segments in our society has diverted from keeping the American patriotism and started to follow some fictional and disturbing lifestyles. At such times, we are required to check our thoughts and the choices of our rulers and maybe realize that mankind is falling in error. That's why rebellions occur; for the simple facts that people seek correction.

4. The Muhammadan swamp

NOTE: This century strictly explains Prophet Muhammad actions. If you find this century uninteresting, please skip to the next 5th century.

Is it appropriate to randomly target Muhammadans and Muslims?

It is not necessary to randomly target Muslims or Islamists unless they commit wrongful acts. Indiscriminate wars don't work. As the Islamic rebels are terrorizing the world, combating Islam indiscriminately will cause many mad, sick and violent Muslims to retaliate vigorously against the Red Nations. Dr. Charles Krauthammer, a political analyst, was asked about the lone wolves problem and he said that it's "the new nightmare". Thousands of lone wolves are after the Red Nations today. The Islamic lone wolves and such sudden attacks can be seen from many angles. From one angle, we tend to see that most lone wolves are unstable emotionally and suffer from psychological problems. One of the main reasons for an average young Muslim to turn into a lone wolf is the political conflicts throughtout the Islamic world.

Political corruption is one of the central causes of the Islamic rebellion. A lone wolf might sympathaize with the victims of unjust societies of the Muslim world and deal with it by committing a violent attack. Though the 9/11 attacks were conducted by a group of trained jihadists, today, those jihadists become seen as role models for the lone wolves. The 9/11 attacks encouraged and brought forth many more sick, mad and violent Muslims to join the Islamic rebelling movement and wage jihad, terror and war on what they call the Crusaders and hostile Zionists. An Islamic sympathizer nowadays might find it encouarging to act in the same manner and attack on his own. If jihad symapthizer is against a certain party, then the person might rebel and strike out of no where, just like the San Bernardino terrorist couple. Financial and social problems, as well as religious extremsim will increase the risk.

As mentioned before, such individuals usually feel enslaved by the current life routine and rebel in return. Some lone wolves have left manifestos that show signs of mental and psychologial wear and stress. We wonder why once a while such young Muslims go on a rampage and attack their "infidel targets and opponents" as they call them. Social problems, poverty and emotional strain increases the risk for mad

The Muhammadan swamp

Muslims of becoming lone wolves. The term *sick person* would better describe such lone wolf cases. An Islamic lone wolf obviously is a person sick of life that is mad at the world and revolts against his or her opposition, and violence is a tool he or she will use to accomplish his or her goals. Since terror attacks have worked well for them, they will continue using them and other methods to reach their goals and desires.

The world may defeat terrorism, but not by indiscriminate wars. Iraq was the wrong beehive to poke. As the 9/11 attacks were an act of war; Iraq never recovered from its war's results. According to Mercer, the largest human resource consulting firm, the Iraqi capital Baghdad has the worst living quality in the world due to the result of the 2003 war. We need to figure out how to diagnose the symptom instead of sending our troops to fight for wrongful reasons. We have to clean the governments of the incompetence and contain the contagious disease of war. Iraq developed the same problems that Syria is suffering from: both were divided as the jihadists took over the lands. Who's the jihadists' next victim? Jordan? Turkey? Saudi Arabia? Iran? India? It's all possible.

Consider the overall situation

Let's say that there are some homeless people that could be starving, and we're not doing enough to help them; isn't that a danger that is threatening everyone else? Just because someone is homeless and begging for help peacefully doesn't mean that he or she won't eventually lose their mind and end up stealing what they need! The homeless is practicing self-control and accepting what he or she is experiencing. In the same manner, millions of poor Muslims are restraining themselves from violence and aggression. It is visible that they practice self-discipline, and they do it out of kindness, not weakness. The opposite can be seen with the rebelling Muslims who kill gruesomely nowadays, after experiencing some financial problems. They eventually can lose it.

The madness disease could be contagious. We have to look at the bigger picture of our current conditions as well. A wise man would suggest: do not become mean and mad. Purify yourself. Love the enemy, if possible, because wars may not solve the problems permanently.

The philosopher

Learning is one of the greatest skills that humans have mastered. Prophet Muhammad was a man who learned from history. Obviously, he managed to establish an empire within 23 years, which surely took him lots of learning and effort to accomplish. The Arabian Emperor Muhammad, the initiator of the first Islamic State, started it as a theological philosophy to promote his Sharia laws and religious ideas. His theological philosophy advanced rapidly within his society, where he found followers and established his community of Muslims within a short period of time, and his philosophy was definitely to change the world. Today, his philosophy is called the religion of Islam.

Roman Empire

The Roman Empire was Muhammad's greatest challenge. He faced that reality quite strangely; as he ended up developing a solution to beat the Roman Empire by producing a new theology. For the Arabs, the Romans' actions were severe and concerning. The Romans had the largest empire and the most power during Muhammad's life.

Nero, the Roman Emperor, did gruesome acts to the Christians: he fed them to lions, killed some of Jesus's apostles, and even tried to abolish Christianity. That was only one of the many emperors who ravaged others in order to control them and hold power over them.

The Romans used to persecute the pious and enslave the weak, as they considered themselves a superior human race. Muhammad proved that he was determined to end the recklessness by the Romans, who flooded the Middle East at that time. It is very obvious that Muhammad was intelligent, driven by rational, not emotions.

A genius

Let's go through what the Muslims claim that Muhammad did to accomplish his mission. Muhammad, purportedly, used his knowledge. From his teen years, he learned politics and diplomatic relations during the tribal wars. Through the years and decades, Muhammad picked up wisdom and became a good communicator and a poet. He wrote the Quran. He became literate and enjoyed the concurrent knowledge of other civilizations. Supposedly, Muhammad accepted and agreed with whatever came to him, unless it was some devious or malicious acts. He could've been an impressive leader for his followers to accept his habits and apply his traditions. He disagreed with those who oppressed the weak as he got older in age. He disapproved conflicts without justifiable reasons. The tribal wars within the Arab tribes were all over the place, and the weak people were looking for a miracle to come and save them from the aggressors. And the Romans of Damascus were the main ones, in his view. The Romans were steadily pushing the Arabs out of Canaan into the deserts of Arabia since they would not submit to the Romans rule nor were willing to pay taxes. The Arabs had no civil rights under Roman rule. On the contrary, when Muhammad was picked to rule and lead the community, he put in place a constitution that gave rights to everybody which supposedly treated all people equally and protected them under the law of the city: Yathrib's constitution. Such actions surely have empowered him at the time. More about his stand with the lower classes will be discussed in next coming quatrains.

<u>A unique philosopher</u>

No one goes to war unless he or she expects to gain more than he or she expects to lose. Hitler, for example, would've never started the second world war unless he expected to gain a lot more than he eventually lost. Supposedly, Muhammad never enjoyed wars but they were necessary to deal with the wealthy tyrants and tribal men. His state resisted the capitalism of the wealthy tribal men and proposed Islamic socialism for everyone that came to join his monotheist campaign. He and his men started the jihad and strived for freedom, which would last for a long time until this day. The current jihad formation was restarted by Osama Bin Laden, who also called for a socialist Islamic country that would adopt all the Muslims and accept them under one umbrella. Bin Laden tried to use the same method as Muhammad by uniting the Arabs and get them to beat the opposition by defeating them militarily. *Jihad* means to strive and put in effort. Whether by fighting physically for an Islamic liberation or by spreading Islam in a peaceful manner, the jihad's goal is to make the people accept Islam as a social norm and submit with the rest of the followers.

Muhammad produced a polity with a monotheist doctrine, and he enforced equality and socialism, and created a socialist conservative society that would offer a united, prosperous and strong community. Today, Islam extends all over the Old World, and Muslims make up a quarter of the world's population. Muslims, for most the part, still follow and live according to the same conservative lifestyle that Muhammad brought in his Islamic philosophy about 1,500 years ago.

The Muhammadan swamp

An orphan introducing socialism

As mentioned before, Muhammad was raised by strangers and casual members of the family such as cousins and uncles. But still, he went from an illiterate nomad and a shepherd to a traveling trader of the ancient civilizations. As he grew, he began accompanying trade caravans and became an accountant and a broker, which turned him into a wealthy merchant who became aware of the social human-error.

The wealthy were degrading the weak and living in ignorance as if they were wild animals. Muhammad found himself on a mission to create a better community, with civil rights and social security for all. Supposedly, he grew up to be a mindful man, just like Abraham, who realized that the government of Nimrod was living off the poor; the rich got more power as the poor went down the drain. Muhammad created a system for people who suffered from hunger, sickness and lived in depression; the Islamic socialism. Today, Muhammad's legacy stands even stronger than Buddha's legacy. Muhammad still has people who rebel and follow his way of dealing with their opposition. Today, there are millions of young kids and old women who are struggling with little food, and many die constantly; especially in the southern hemisphere. In the Muslim world, the destitute look up to Muhammad as an icon and a role model to follow. Muhammad's philosophy is a swamp, meant to destroy capitalism and resist hoarding wealth, which millions of Muslims seem to still follow and adore. More about his action regarding the poor will be explained in the "Muhammad and the 99%" quatrain.

Socialist right activists or maniacs?

Just like today's billionaires, Bin Laden was a wealthy man who donated his money, body and soul to revive the Islamic rebellion because he wanted to form a universal Islamic government. Bin Laden specifically wanted to create a government that would provide the best service to all Muslims fairly and equally, just as Muhammad taught in his Islamic philosophy.

Crime follows poverty. If the current poverty level continues, there will never be total peace in the world. Bin Laden did it out of personal faith that he would cause the world to change, and obviously it has, quicker than anticipated. Abraham the Patriarch was also such a rebel, who left his homeland to create a better life for his descendants.

The Muhammadan swamp

Two thousand years after Abraham's time, Jesus Christ found the same problem happening in the land of Israel. The Jews, descendants of Abraham, used to get taxed by the Romans just to be able to worship at their temple. Their chiefs submitted to the Roman rule, and that's why Jesus Christ rebelled using word of mouth, as he criticized the corrupted leaders. In some sense, Muhammad accomplished what Jesus Christ wanted to be done: to kick the Romans out of the Holy Land and give it back to the average humans who simply just wanted food and drink to survive and go on.

Muhammad the servant vs. Jesus the Messiah

Muhammad claimed that he was a servant of God by delivering a divine message. Supposedly, it's the same God that's claimed to be the God of Abraham.

But why would a nomad Arab claim to be God's servant if he's an emperor and chief in command of armed troops? For politics; maybe.

Obviously, in those ancient times, slavery was a common business; even until the 17th century. Muhammad used his strategic intelligence and diplomatic policies to abolish slavery from Arabia; and turn slaves into warriors and soldiers. It is said that Muhammad had wanted to be God's servant before kneeling and submitting to the Romans and becoming one of their fallen slaves and servants.

As the Messiah, Jesus Christ did nothing wrong but warn the concurrent slave owners that they eventually would suffer in life. Jesus Christ has explained that it would be hard for the rich to enter paradise in the next life. So while Jesus warned, Muhammad warred in return.

Back to the creed

Muhammad claimed that his mission was a holy one: to serve the Lord. Abraham's monotheism ideology is regarded as the worshipping of a celestial Godly power, which is claimed to be the supreme Lord of all of the creation.

Purportedly, Muhammad's first wife was a Christian woman who worshipped the God of Jesus Christ, which at first Muhammad was unfamiliar with. He decided that such a God was the master of all that was revealed to him. According to the legends of Islam, Muhammad vowed to serve the Lord after he realized that his duty was a holy mission: to deliver the message to the people about God's holiness and power. Allegedly, Muhammad came to figure that he was God's avenger that was supposed to bring his wrath on the evildoers, which Jesus Christ warned of a few centuries before that time. Supposedly, Archangel Gabriel told Muhammad to do so.

The power of the word

Supposedly at first, Muhammad decided to talk to the people with common sense. When he was a grown man in his forties, he started to tell the people to be kind in treatment and to stop the worship of idols. With a logical consideration of other beings, Muhammad supposedly proposed to end the tradition of honor killings, tribal warfare, greed, ignorance and enslaving the poor. Muhammad is reported to have reasoned with the people about their actions and elaborated with them rationally. It was not long before he faced serious problems with the leaders and rich men as their mischief increased his determination to end their tyranny. Abraham and Moses suffered the same consequence because of their similar Godly teachings; which probably made Muhammad think that he was following the Abrahamic mindset.

Rejecting idols

Supposedly after encountering Archangel Gabriel, Muhammad converted to a full theist like Abraham; he began to believe in God, the creator. He regarded this unknown Lord as "The God, the beneficent, and the merciful," following the same phrasing that King Solomon used.

Muhammad disapproved of using images and idols to worship; he must've learned that idea from the Torah and the commandments of Moses. The jihadists still follow the concept. That's why the Islamic State Caliphate (ISC) has been destroying ancient idols and statues since 2014.

Supposedly, Muhammad preached just as Jesus did, but the only difference is that Muhammad was not a messiah, whereas Jesus was supported by the Holy Spirit. Muslims say that Muhammad's public preaching is what attracted the people, especially the weak and poor. It wasn't long before many approved Muhammad's message and began to follow him, including the sons and brothers of the great merchants and tribal leaders. Even young men of the neighborhood were leaning with him, as fallen civilians and unprotected foreigners praised him. Purportedly, Muhammad affirmed that it was wrong for his followers to praise him to the point that he did not allow anyone to draw his image or picture. Allegedly, he taught to be proud of the Lord, the God that creates things. It's been confirmed that the leaders of his time and wealthy powerful men did not appreciate his teachings at all.

The lesson

According to the Muslims, Muhammad's calls consisted of abandoning evil and having a righteous conscious. He advised everyone to assist others, especially the neighbors. He focused on those in need, especially the orphans. Muhammad rejected cheating and fraud within his community. He opposed coveting wealth and also opposed sexual immorality and disapproved of randomly killing women. Supposedly, calls against female abuse were the necessary step that caused many women to follow him. According to some sources, those women are the ones who later warned him against whoever plotted against him, planned to assassinate him, or decided to strike him, as those women secretly helped him to perform his mission. He opposed the honor killing of young girls, so that could've been very attractive to women who lost their daughters to such honor killings. Regardless, anyone who is righteous and virtuous usually finds support from others.

When Muhammad began to preach to the public in Mecca, which also is claimed to be the birthplace of Ishmael son of Abraham, the prominent public figures ignored him at first.

Those scenarios played a role in how his followers vowed to him and made him gain popularity. Persecution usually has little effect on the growth of a party. Muhammad's followers grew in number, and the threat to the local tribal rulers and trade leaders made them worried about being overthrown, so they eventually tried to reason with him.

Muhammad against the capitalists

Prophet Muhammad must've been a tactical strategist because he surely was working through a process—planned and executed carefully. Purportedly, he preached as any priest, rabbi or imam, but the difference is that his preaching was just a step in the process to come afterward. Even though the leaders and rich men ignored him at first, many of his followers liked his teachings and began to change.

The rich men and leaders mocked him after a while, while he started gaining support and favoritism by the poor and fallen civilians. Eventually, after a few years, those rich men and tribal leaders started to defy him. Soon enough, the clash turned into physical transgression, as he refused to stop his teachings. They ended up harming Muhammad and whoever followed him or agreed with his philosophy.

By the time those powerful men tried to fix the problem, it was too late. Muhammad had warned them that it was too late, as they had misused and abused their powers already. The more they tried to reason with him, the more he was becoming convinced that what he was doing was the right thing. Muhammad became determined to end the oppression as his conscience pushed him. He claimed that the Archangel Gabriel told him to do so. At times, he claimed that he wasn't going to quit on his Lord and get punished like Jonas of Nineveh. Jonas was an ancient Babylonian prophet, who fled from God and then got cursed for deserting the duty.

Wealth, women, leadership

According to Islam, at some point the tribal leaders tried to reason with Muhammad and offered him leadership if he wished, any money he requested, and any women he wanted. Supposedly, they just wanted him to quit his teachings and change his message which disturbed their political powers within the society.

Those offers seemed attractive, but allegedly he refused to quit on the Lord or bow down before idols and side with the apostates and idolaters. The wealthy and powerful men ended up standing against him and opposed his followers. They even provoked physical conflict by killing and torturing members of Muhammad's movement and his Muslim community. Eventually, there were many murder attempts on his life.

The counter response

While Muhammad was preaching with direct words and solid acts, his opposition was busy torturing, persecuting and plotting against his followers. It was such events that caused the matter to become personal to Muhammad rather than a Godly duty. It became a personal problem to Muhammad when there was an assassination attempt on his life right at home while sleeping in his bed room, which also failed.

Killing Muhammad was not very easy, but it forced him to depart his hometown and move to Yathrib, known today as Medina. That's where he was able to establish his caliphate and create his law and philosophy by forming the structure of his polity, where he reshaped the future of his people. Arabia was the lower part of the Middle East, and that's what made its location become significant. It became the heart of the Islamic rebellion, as it expanded east, west, north, and south of that city after he became the leader of Yathrib. That was fourteen hundred years ago. Today it is still the city of Muhammad which celebrates his philosophy and creed as the main one in that land.

Muhammad's spirituality

Muhammad claimed that everything was spiritual. Therefore, perfection is the only way to succeed in life, to reach a better state, and hopefully the perfect condition that Abraham the Patriarch was devoted to reaching. Muhammad had used the exact same myth in his new theology that he was coming up with.

Allegedly, Muhammad didn't reject the Torah of Moses or the Gospel of Jesus. Better yet, he used the same ideologies and used Hammurabi's code of ethics in his polity. Hammurabi was a lawmaker of Babylon about 3,500 years ago. Hammurabi's code is the law that could be explained by the "an eye for an eye" discipline model. But according to Muhammad, at the end of the day, God is the main spiritual judge.

Plato's model of direct democracy was brought into work by Muhammad in his new polity, which came to existence a thousand years after Plato existed. Muhammad built a mosque, and that's where it all happened between the people and their leadership. Thus, he combined state and religion into one. That's how he mixed the monotheist creed into his political statehood: the Islamic caliphate.

Prophet's mission vs. an insane philosopher

Muhammad's approach included a very strict philosophical element while combining spirituality, statesmanship, civil law, and human resources efficiently. It meant to bring in a self-motivated unity for the average civilians to create a powerful social society. He believed that it was the best way to obtain a perfect community. Therefore, mankind will never be completely satisfied until all the struggles of life are resolved. That's when mankind will go back to their original state of a perfect existence. Supposedly, the best way to reach perfection is to understand and balance the spirituality within the state and community.

The Muhammadan swamp

Muhammad claimed that humans have three separate spirits all within one body: an angel, the self, and a demon, who all reside in the human's body. It's the same philosophy as Aristotle, who claimed that humans contain three souls: the vegetative soul, the sensitive soul, and the rational soul. The vegetative soul could be seen as an angel, the sensitive soul could be seen as a demon, and the rational soul, which could be seen as the self.

A reformed Jewish theology

This vital combination of ideas that Muhammad was coming up with was a part of a long-term jihad against oppression. He appreciated those who rebel and strive for perfection. It gave Muhammad the ability to form the Caliph's position in his community. It's the same way George Washington contributed in the forming of the presidency, which enabled a common individual to take the lead and rule the nation.

The perfect way to put Muhammad's philosophy into words is that his religious order can be seen as a lower-class Jewish theology. His move seemed as if he was a reformer who came up with another form of Judaism. Muhammad reformed the ancient Jewish ideology to make his new Abrahamic faith by submitting to the God of Abraham. Muhammad took Muslims to a lower submission level according to his philosophy, where he encouraged his followers to strive for more. He encouraged bowing down to the ground and to stay humble and take the land as a pillow. In other words, Muhammad was more like a Jew who accepted Jesus Christ as the Messiah and made a new dogma.

A Muslim's first pillar is to testify to the oneness of the Lord, the one and absolute God of Abraham. Again, Jews also believed in one God, the peace, the highest, and the God of Abraham. *Elohim* is the Hebrew term for God; *Allah* is the Arabic word for God. The God is supposed to be the unknown, unseen, and undefeatable power and supreme Lord.

How it went

Here's how Muhammad's reformed philosophy compared with Judaism's aspect of worship which Moses remodeled:

Worship:

Mandatory prayers go as the following. The believers in the God of Abraham, as Muhammad's theology described, were advised to pray five times a day, while Judaism instructs to perform three prayers per day. Obviously, Muhammad pushed the Muslims to go further and perform two extra daily prayers.

Alms:

Muhammad mandated the Sadaqah in his Islamic review, which meant a voluntary charity that is due to the poor. In the same notion, Judaism ascribed the Tzedakah on the followers, which means justice and is used to signify charity and donations, which is a practice that Jews are required to carry out. Judaism mandates to donate a portion of their income to charitable institutions or to any needy people as taught in the Hebrew Bible. Maimonides, an ancient rabbi and a scholar provided more details regarding the Jewish Tzedakah.

Fasting:

For Jews, fasting means abstaining completely from food and drink, including water for six days of the year. Muhammad, the founder of Islam depended on the lunar calendar to fast a full lunar month, which is either 28 or 29 days. In Islam, Muslims are obligated to practice fasting during the month of Ramadan from dawn until sunset. Muslims are prohibited from eating, drinking, smoking, and engaging in sexual activity.

Laws of Islam vs. Jewish laws:

Because Muhammad was born in Arabia, he shared Judaism's origin as both came out of the Middle East, as both religions are considered to be Abrahamic creeds. Muhammad upgraded many aspects from Judaism in his religion of Islam, as Muhammad was strongly influenced by Judaism in its fundamental religious outlook, structure, jurisprudence and technical practice.

Judaism and Islam are similar by having unique systems of religious laws, where Muhammad's law is the Sharia (legislation), and Judaism's law is the Halakha. Both Judaism and Islam consider the study of religious laws to be a form of worship.

Judaism and Islam support Hammurabi's code for justice. He was a Babylonian statesman that invented the law back in the 1700s BC. He's the one who made the first retaliatory punishment, which is known today as the Hammurabi Code. As mentioned, he was the one who provided the eye-for-an-eye method of disciplinary action. Some have claimed that Hammurabi was an Israelite from Abraham's progeny.

The Muhammadan swamp

Differing from Christianity:

When comparing Islam and Judaism, we find that neither religion subscribes to the concept of the original sin as Christianity does. Judaism practices circumcision for males, and Muhammad ordered his followers to circumcise, as it is considered an Abrahamic duty. Eating swine flesh was prohibited by Muhammad; in the same way the Judaism implements that notion.

Muhammad's faith agreed with Judaism, where both consider the Christian doctrine of the Trinity and the belief of Jesus Christ being as a God to be explicitly against the tenets of monotheism. In the Abrahamic creed, God is one, and worshipping other objects is idolatry because the worship of graven images is likewise forbidden. Muhammad's philosophy consists of angels and demons, just as Judaism taught.

No man from the Hebrews or Israelites was able to come forth and extract out of Judaism and form a new monotheist nation as Muhammad did. Muhammad could've been as a Jewish Rabbi that developed a new philosophy, which enabled him to label himself as a monotheist. More likely, he was a follower of Judaism with a reformed, organized, and rational theology. Better yet, the truth is that Islam was nothing but a philosophy that Muhammad put to the test. Here we are, 1,400 years later, and we can see that his philosophy has prevailed as his system rocked the world more than any other prophets' ever did. Just looking at the current Islamic rebellion and jihadism is the best proof.

Muhammad's role

Muhammad was a nomad who transformed into a sudden philosopher, who was promoted to a chief and then to a judge who eventually became a general of war. Finally, Muhammad became the commander in chief after he produced the Islamic caliphate. He provided the Islamic thought and mentality, which solidified his philosophy, through the continuation of the caliphate, which means the *succession to the mission*. After all that, he created his state and implied the prophetic role to it, where he then wished to be called Muhammad, the messenger of the God.

A lesson to learn from

Today, the world still struggles with violence and aggression.

The Muhammadan swamp

Islam is the philosophy of one man, Muhammad, who built his case on the faults of those who existed before him, which enabled him to succeed and go on to lead. Islam, by now, is followed by one-fourth of the world's population. Today, we have 1.7+ billion Muslims who claim to belong to the Muhammadan sect, which he reformed and guided. In the end, allegedly righteous virtue, fair treatment, and a little theology enabled him to get the job done.

For the God

As for the God, who is claimed by the Islamic community to be the head of everything, many Muslims believe that they have submitted to him. Therefore, they hold Muhammad as an enlightened man. Muslims believe that they are following Muhammad on a path to perfection, which is supposedly the only way to go or otherwise live in ignorance.

Islam, the rebellious duty

The major influence that is motivating the current jihadists to rebel and drag other Muslims along with them is defined by how the human civilization has evolved by today. While the lands of the Arabs contain over 50% of the worldly oil reserves, the instructions by the Muslim priests and imams who call for jihad adds fuel to the fire, just like the unemployment and social struggles of the Middle East do. The Islamic world finally is creating generations of rebels who can connect from all around the world. It's what Big Laden initiated: to move militias and conduct armed operations on a massive scale which can be seen today in Syria and Iraq. By now, one-fourth of the world's population is under the influence of those rebelling calls. Every time foreign governments and authorities interfere between the Muslims and their issues, calling for jihad kicks off right away by the imams and preachers.

Today, many Muslims feel that they had been violated since the early 1900s, when the British overran the Ottoman caliphate and took over the Middle East, as it allowed the Jews to establish the State of Israel in 1948. Evidently, Muslims and Arabs must be mad and fed up. That's why we see young Muslims come out to rebel and commit jihad harder than ever before. Again, it's the same old Arabic dream that fuels the fire.

Comparing Muhammad and Moses

From Jews to Muslims, the only evidence that we have about the two creeds is the scripts and the written information that we have. We only have the Torah that Moses brought to the Egyptian-Hebrew people, who later became known as Jews and the Quran that was brought by Muhammad to the nomad people of Saudi Arabia, who later came to be known as Muslims. The Jews then formed the Kingdom of Israel, and the Muhammadans were able to create the Islamic caliphate that evolved into an Islamic Empire within a few centuries. Both Muhammad and Moses claimed to be far distant sons of Abraham the Patriarch, as both of them claimed to be serving the God of Abraham. Both Jews and Muslims follow their prophetic doctrines, the monotheist beliefs that instruct to strive for the sake of God, as Moses and Muhammad tried. Both were rebels in action, where they led great religious rebellions to bring change to their people, and both have affected the world, where Muslims and Jews are the followers of those two men. Muhammad and Moses claimed to have done a holy duty, to bring the peoples' attention to God or otherwise face harsh punishments and barbaric, idle lives. Barbarism leads to evil, which comes from idle hands, as empty hands are the devil's playground, as some say. This makes it clear why the Islamists and Zionists clash; they're two cousins at war over their forefather Abraham's inheritance and prophecy.

Ultimately

Regardless of the authenticity of Muhammad's prophethood or how righteous his state was or how effective his laws were or how successful his philosophy was, his ideology of running a civil society using the Islamic doctrine is still praised by the millions of Muslims of our time. The Muhammadan ideology is the most significant philosophy out of all the theologies that are being used and practiced by the people today.

Today, Islam is regarded as an Abrahamic faith, regardless of Muhammad's legitimacy as a prophet. Whether Muhammad was a prophet or simply a successful politician is not the question in our case; his philosophy still is very powerful and is growing rapidly, as we see today.

Apparently, for many historians, the ancient biblical prophecies are coming true. The holy wars and the great battles have been taking place since the 6th century. From Andalusia to Constantinople, Jerusalem and Carthage, even Rome and Alexandrea, since Prophet Muhammad came out, the holy wars and Islamic rebellions have reached or conquered them one after another. And let's keep in mind that by the 21st century, Osama Bin Laden had revived the Islamic rebellion and its attacks had reached New York City. Even Paris, London, Sydney, Copenhagen and more western cities have been attacked since then. And surely the 9/11 attacks are what made Osama Bin Laden the most publicized Islamic warrior to date.

The Muhammadan swamp

Muhammad's philosophy is a massive swamp that he has left behind for the people to come across. Millions of people have embraced it and they call themselves Muslims. The Islamic socialism doctrine that he has left behind has found many adherents and followers throughout the Old World. That's why the Muslims glorify Muhammad's rebellious ideology so much. They do so for the simple fact that hundreds of millions Muslims are poor and weak. Most Muslims live in the Old World, specifically in the southern hemisphere. Thus, the Muhammadan swamp will always bring forth mad and violent Muslims who will fight and try to revive his main legacy; the caliphate. They do so in order to gain their ultimate goal which a monotheist political state, which would apply an Islamic socialism model of social justice for all the Muslims worldwide, using the Quran for its constitution and the Sharia law for its legislation.

5. After the collapse of the Ottoman caliphate
Muhammad's legacy revived: the caliphate

Looking at the polity that Muhammad created in the 6th century until the day that his caliphate was abolished in the 1920s, it seems that randomly casual Muslims strived for the *one Islamic central government*. Muhammad himself, until he started the caliphate in Yathrib, was not a significant character and suddenly became a leader after he formed his socialist democratic constitutional caliphate during the 6th century.

The caliphate's democracy was deployed through the 'majority wins' system, as people followed through a political system and electoral protocols. A head chairman that represents the council is also elected and is called the caliph, which translates to "the successor." Some caliphs renamed the title to *emir al-mumineen* (nation prince) and *sultan* (governor). Actually, it was more like an emperor's role because once the caliph is selected; he stays in office until death. The caliph is more like an elected king since the caliph is also the commander in chief of the armed forces. Comparing to the American president, whose duty is temporary and can be limited to eight years in two terms, the caliph is selected to be a permanent commander. The caliph is an elected emperor, and the caliphate is more like an Islamic republic, following the Sunni Islamic prophetic doctrine of Muhammad. Basically it's a socialist theocracy.

Of course, at that time it wasn't a massive empire. But according to that system, as much as one-quarter of today's human population would fall under such authority, which is roughly 1.7 billion people. That's ten times the size of the former Islamic caliphate, where the Ottoman Empire had anywhere from 140-170 million citizens by the early 1900s.

Wars and breakdown of the former Ottoman caliphate

Of course, the Ottoman Empire's involvement in World War I contributed to its total collapse. The Ottomans lost a lot of power, as their arrogance and greed drained them. Their end was deadly, and their whole history became catastrophic. The last Ottoman sultan was kicked out and sent to exile in France along with his family.

The remnants of that empire are still here: modern day Turks and Arabs. They're still engulfed with trouble and haven't been able to

After the collapse of the Ottoman caliphate

recover from their former fallen empire. Today, ninety years later, we witness the horrible consequences of the breakdown of the Ottoman Empire. The Middle Eastern Muslims are still fighting over power. The Jews were able to establish a democratic authority, Israel, but it also is still having a lot of internal problems. All those are the results of the Ottomans and what they left behind, the remnants that have not been able to catch up with modern civilizations to settle their differences.

Since the breakdown of the Ottoman caliphate, many Muslims around the world have been calling to revive such an Islamic political municipality. Since the abolishment of the former caliphate, the calls for jihad by the imams have increasingly been taking place all over the Islamic world. The establishment of the Jewish-Zionist backed state, Israel, and the jihad calls have intensified the flames of the war. Islam, as a rebellious philosophy, encourages the Muslims to rebel against oppression and aggression in the same manner Abraham the Patriarch did. That's why Bin Laden supported the rebellion financially, which enabled the Islamic rebelling movement to grow in power and strength. After Bin Laden formed Al-Qaeda in 1988, the intensity of the jihading project doubled, if not tripled. Basically every time a caliphate is eliminated, other Muslims strive to create another one. Since the former Ottoman caliphate was abolished, the Muslims in the Middle East have created nations other than what would be seen as Islamic caliphates.

New Formation for the Muslims

As the Ottoman caliphate was dismantled, Mustafa Kamal Atatürk formed Turkey and became its president. The Arabs formed Iraq, Syria, Jordan, Lebanon, Saudi Arabia, Kuwait, Yemen, Oman, UAE, Qatar, Bahrain and Egypt, and used the Sykes-Picot dividing lines as the borders of the countries and were approved by the UN.

Some of those countries were turned into republics, while some became kingdoms and others became sultanates. But undoubtedly, most of them fell in the grips of dictators and tyrants, as the Arabs were left behind, screwed by the British colonization, which left the Middle East in such horrible conditions after the Brits demolished the Ottoman government that controlled the Middle East.

After the collapse of the Ottoman caliphate

New formation for the Jews

There was a gentleman from Jewish descent born in 1886 in Poland known as Mr. David Ben Gurion, who later became known as Israel's founding father. David Ben Gurion was an ambitious Zionist who was able to establish the Jewish State of Israel after the Ottoman's rule collapsed and fell into the hands of the Brits. Ben Gurion was a brilliant Jew who strived to establish the new Jewish homeland in the land of Palestine, which consisted of Tel Aviv and its surroundings. The main movement that helped to build the Jewish state was the Zionist movement, which existed even before Ben Gurion was born. They initiated their own colony and assembled a government that regulated the area and became an independent Jewish state recognized by the United Nations and the United States of America as well.

Zionist irredentism

Irredentism attributes to any political or social movement that aims to repossess or retake a lost homeland. Zionism refers to a nationalist and a political movement that consists mostly of Jews and some others, who support the reestablishment of a Jewish state as homeland in the territory that's defined as the historic land of Israel.

The Zionist party originally was a Jewish liberation movement, and generally aimed for the repatriation of a dispersed socio-religious group to what the Zionists see as the abandoned homeland of the Jews that they abandoned about a thousand years ago due to the wars and persecution against them in the past.

The Zionist claim is based on an ancient ancestral inhabitance, theologically rooted in a mosaic cosmogony. That's where the problem comes in place because Jerusalem is a holy site for the Muslims also. Since 1948, the Islamic world has felt that its dignity has been attacked, as they feel that some dishonor has touched Islam due to the Holy Land's conflict.

The original Israel – Jacob

The name Israel was given to Jacob, son of Isaac, Abraham's grandson, who resided in the land of Canaan and Palestine about 4,000 years ago. Israel (Jacob) had thirteen children, twelve of them who were boys that became the origin of Bani Israel (Sons of Israel). Bani Israel was the tribe that contributed and gave birth to Judaism following the death of their fathers, Isaac and Abraham. More details and full descriptions of the legends are found in the first five chapters of the Holy Bible (www.BibleGateway.com).

Zionism today is a movement that consists of many nationalities and people of many religions. Jewish people shouldn't be confused with Zionists, who were given that name after mount Zion in Jerusalem, where King Solomon's temple stood on 3,000 years ago. King Solomon, as mentioned before, is the son of King David, the Israelite King, who indeed formed the first Jewish state ever. Zion refers to a hill in Jerusalem, on which stood a Philistine fortress that was conquered by King David after he killed Goliath, the giant as documented in the ancient legend of the Hebrews. His son, Solomon, built a temple instead of the fortress and it became known as the 1st temple.

The Zionists were striving for the Jewish dream, which is to conquer the land of Palestine and establish a homeland, which they accomplished in 1948, and the country became known as the State of Israel. Thus, the name Israel refers to the land that Jacob once inhabited.

Modern day Israel

The modern State of Israel was established as a Jewish state by the Zionists in 1948. Its Law of Return grants the right of citizenship to any Jew by ancestry who requests it. According to the Jewish tradition, Jewish ancestry is traced back to the Biblical Patriarch Abraham, to his son Isaac, and Abraham's grandson Jacob, who was renamed Israel. The Jewish people today are an ethnoreligious group, that's claimed to have originated from the historical Israelite tribes (Bani Israel), who at some point abandoned the land of Israel and went into diaspora.

Today, there are around 15 million Jews worldwide. Six million reside in Israel, five million live in the United States and the rest are scattered all throughout the world.

The 1948 exodus

Since David Ben Gurion announced the independence of Israel, there has been massive turmoil between the Zionists and the nationalist Arabs who were living in the area, as hundreds of thousands of Jews flocked to Israel during the 1948 exodus. In response, the Arabs joined the Baath Arabic Socialist Party, to build an Arab nation in the Middle East. The Baath party and Mr. Aflaq's involvement and admiration of

After the collapse of the Ottoman caliphate

the Arabic nationalism will be explained in the next quatrains.

Even though the continuous conflict has been going on for the past 70 years, many Jews around the world are being harassed, while few millions of them took advantage of Israel's law of return and moved back to their homeland.

Regardless of the Jews and how much they're involved in the state of Israel, the Zionists are the main target of the jihad. It's fair to say that the Zionist movement and its actions have fired back on the Jewish community, which is still taking hits here and there. The main reason of Zionism was to end anti-Semitism. Instead, the Zionists actions have fired back on the Jews which were something that was unpredictable.

What's Holy and what's not?

While God Almighty was considered to be the only Holy being, nowadays the term Holy Lands is given to the area surrounding Jerusalem as well. After all the bloodshed in that area, truly, it feels as if it's an unholy piece of land. Jews, Muslims and even Christians claim that Jerusalem is a holy land since Abraham the Patriarch found his peace there after departing from his hometown Ur, as mentioned before.

Again, Muslims holds Abraham as the first father of Islam, and Jews also claim to be descendants of his grandson, Jacob. Christians believe that Jesus Christ, the Israelite descendant of King David, is the Messiah and also believe that he's God's spirit manifested. Muslims also believe that Jerusalem is the land of Jesus Christ, who they considered the Messiah of humanity. The idea is rejected by the Jews. The notion that Jesus Christ, son of Virgin Mary, from King David's progeny, is the Messiah is a concept that's totally rejected by the Jews. Judaism disagrees with that specific idea, as they have their own Moshiach (Messiah) that they're waiting for. So basically, Christians and Muslims are awaiting the return of Jesus Christ to come and take leadership of the world, while, on the other hand, the Jews disagree with that belief. By now, it's all tangled up. So what is Holy? And what is not? We'll leave it for others to decide.

Facts

While the State of Israel claims that it's a Jewish state, half of the Israelis nowadays identify themselves secular people. But Israel's claim that it's a Jewish state gives the Muslims an impression that they have the right to a global Islamic Caliphate, the same way Muhammad left it back

After the collapse of the Ottoman caliphate

in the 6th century and which Bin Laden called and strived for.

The current caliphate (ISC) was revived in 2014 and is on the move to bring back the global caliphate. Prophet Muhammad is claimed to be the initiator of the first Islamic caliphate. The Islamic State Caliphate (ISC) holds the founding father, Prophet Muhammad, as the icon, which tends to follow his laws and implement his code of philosophy while contesting Abraham's spiritual faith of monotheism.

A turning point

Regardless, the jihadist vs. Zionist conflict is solvable. Today's technology is superior to that of the past and many governments have become very powerful and dominant. The New York Stock Exchange is a great example of our technological advancement. Since Prophet Muhammad's time and his creation of the caliphate in the 6th century, more than two thousand cities have been created worldwide, as energy, food, medicine and manufacturing evolved to what we have today.

Today, nuclear scientists can create devices that can wipe out cities of millions of people in a very short time. But as science helped our comfort and eased our lives, inventions like firearms enable anyone, even children, to become very deadly. By now, mankind is capable of doing astounding things. We even hear of children under the age of 12 stealing cars and committing bizarre acts nowadays.

We must focus on improving the future. So we should, as adults, teach our children conclusive common sense. We should make our kids become better teachers, and hopefully they might lead to success instead of becoming grown ups that have been misled, just like some of the current lost generations in the southern hemisphere.

What good do education and knowledge provide for humanity if our fellow humans are abusing and misusing it? What's the point of creating powerful weaponry such as the Russian AK-47, which is an easy-to-get tool that is devastating societies all over the world?

Rich northern-hemisphere, dirty southern-hemisphere

Today, humanity is divided into three categories. First, we have the wealthy who we call the rich northerners, since they live in the northern hemisphere. Then we have the struggling poor nations who live in the southern hemisphere whom we call the dirty south. And then we have middle class nations who fall in between the two mentioned classes.

After the collapse of the Ottoman caliphate

The rich north is given that title because of the wealthy and affluent people and nations that live in the northern hemisphere.

The dirty south is given that title as the people and nations of the southern hemisphere are known to be mostly poor. Most people who live in South America, South Asia, and South of the Mediterranean are poor. In Africa, some nations are still living in their dark ages.

After the Ottomans collapsed

Nations are still being formed, and as mentioned before, many nations in Africa are still fighting for sovereignty, independence and freedom.

When an authority of a nation collapses, the enforcement of law stops, and corruption starts to take place. When a nation is left behind and its people are ignored; political, social and financial problems develop and grow, and in such situations people usually rebel and revolt. That's how it is in the Islamic world today since the Ottomans collapsed.

Once the Ottoman regime collapsed in the early 1900s, the civilians were left to struggle until they were able to form new nations and governments. Since then, the Arabization of the many ethnicities of the Middle East has been occurring increasingly; especially by hardcore Arab dogmatists such as the Baathists. But now we have an Islamization movement taking place, which the Islamists are trying to achieve. The current caliphate (ISC) is trying to form an Islamic nation that consists of all ethnicities. Being an Arab is totally different from being a Muslim. Since the collapse of the Ottoman Empire, many Middle Easterners are still struggling to find their sense of nationality.

Introducing socialism

Regarding the economic class, most Middle Eastern people fall between rich and poor. But certain Arab countries, such as Qatar and Kuwait, are extremely rich due to the massive oil preserves they have.

The collapse of the Ottoman Empire gave rise to the Baath Party, which is an Arabic socialist party that was involved in the politics of the Middle East since the 1940s. The Baath Arabic Socialist Party was founded by Michel Aflaq, a Syrian philosopher, who was educated in France and then went on to teach young Arabs about unity, liberty and socialism. The Baath Party also helped Saddam Hussein rise to power, and also influenced millions of Arabs who lived in the Middle East.

After the collapse of the Ottoman caliphate

Michel Aflaq studied in Europe during the 1930s. He was pretty familiar with modern governance, which he brought with him to the Baath Arabic Socialist Party. He was impressed with how Hitler came to power. Aflaq had a vision for the Arab world to be united under one banner, the same way Hitler tried to unite Europe under his Nazi state. Even though he was a devout Christian, Aflaq is seen as the champion and savior of the Arabic world. It was the beginning of the Arabization.

Michel Aflaq expressed that Arabic socialism has come in place because of the need. Many young and eager Arabs liked his philosophy as he gained the support of millions of educated young Arabs. Even though the Arabs failed at forming a United Arabic Republic (the Arabic dream), they kept their Arabism and made several Arab nations.

Arabic resurrection

Aflaq also recruited Saddam Hussein to the Arabic Party, which inspired Saddam and helped him rise and shine. Under Saddam Hussein's regime, education was a free privilege to all Arabs. Hussein's regime mandated that refusing to send a child to school at the age of six was a crime. The system was in place starting from the 1970s until he was removed from office in '03. The law included females as well.

The word *Baath* means 'resurrection.' Saddam Hussein's Baathist government scholarships were given every year for thousands of Arabs to study abroad. This resulted in a robust education system that enjoyed a positive reputation and made Iraq the destination for many Arab students in the region, who also glorified the free education that the Baath party offered. Saddam wanted to produce tough Arabs. Resurrecting the Arab world was the Baathist main goal.

The main goal of the Baath Socialist Arabic Party was to resurrect the Arabic unity and create a class of educated striving Arab nationalists, and they sure did. The Caliph Abu Bakr Al-Baghdadi, founder of the Islamic State Caliphate (ISC), earned his Ph.D. in the Islamology field of studies from the University of Baghdad and is class of the year 2000. Abu Bakr Al-Baghdadi also is known as Al-Baghdadi II, is a professional Islamic scholar who earned his education by the Baathists' regime education system under Saddam Hussein's leadership, which taught and encouraged the Arabs to dominate the Middle East. That's what the Baathist party built: the revolutionary mentality for the Arabs.

After the collapse of the Ottoman caliphate

By the 1990s, under Saddam Hussein, Iraq had thousands of scholars and scientists, which empowered the Iraqi culture and revived the Arabic nation's educated classes. Even though Saddam Hussein had many opponents, most Iraqis didn't oppose nor rebel against him as much as in other Arab countries, such as Saudi Arabia or Yemen. While Saddam was investing into his nation by providing welfare and education, the Saudi monarchy was and still fuels the hate and madness by providing social restraint, which causes the Saudis to rebel and go out of control. From another standpoint, Osama Bin Laden wished to turn Saudi Arabia into another Iraq. This stimulation is described in next centuries and quatrains.

A conscientious mission

It is our duty to intectually conquer the world and start finding ways to save the children before the world reaches a point of no return. The problem has to do with employment, where a nation needs farmers and workers to feed and help the teachers and scholars in return. In the Middle East, todays' unemployment, excessive poverty, and political power struggles is causing millions of people to fall behind. Just to mention, we have seen this issue also occur in Mexico since the 1800s.

All humans dream of their independent and happy state of being; which we call the American dream. But people have necessities and priorities in life, and those needs need to be filled and should be the number one concern on the UN's checklist.

Face on

We need to face the problems that humanity struggles with at some point. Humanity is one community, regardless of race, religion, gender, age, color or shape. A leader is responsible for the problems that are inflicted upon his nation under his watch. What's the point of governments if they neglect the poor within their nations?

Unfortunately, leaders usually want good mainly for themselves and care less about the rest. Some leaders see themselves as elites and feel that they shouldn't worry about anyone else. Not every leader is a solid patriot or an honest lover of his nation. All leaders at any position are responsible and should be held accountable for the welfare of their civilians and servants. Each taxpayer should receive better benefits and perfect privileges the same way their rulers and leaders do. The leaders are not better than their people other than the fact that their responsibility is bigger than the average citizen's responsibility. At any given moment, any leader who does not provide enough should be recognized as irresponsible and immediately removed from office.

Politicians and leaders have to provide better development and advance life for their fellow citizens. And the Islamic world is full of political corruption. Saying that affirms that the Islamic rebellion is a situation that can be solved only by the whole world at once. There is no country, or group of people, who can crush the Islamic rebellion. The best that can be done is to have the whole world come together and permanently deal with the actual reality and fix the problem from the inside out. Islamic rebels and jihadists need to be treated from the inside out since their problem starts from within. The Islamic rebels and jihadists feel as if they're about to wage World War III, where they feel as stealthy and energetic as the Nazis were in the 1930s and 1940s. Jihadists are aiming for World War III and trying to drag the world into it as quickly as they can, which would enable Islam to produce the next superpower; if their plan goes well. Osama Bin Laden's words inspired them, much more than Hitler's did on the Germans in the 1930s.

Islamic jihadism

The current jihadism was developed after the collapse of the former Islamic caliphate, which was known as the Ottoman Empire. As mentioned before, the Middle East broke into about 30 separate nations. During the fall of the Ottoman Empire, many sultans called for jihad and some issued legal orders to draft soldiers to join the Islamic armies of the sultan. But they were not answered as much as the calls by the imams of Palestine, once the Israel was being rebuilt. One popular voice was a Middle Eastern imam who, after the collapse of the Ottoman Empire, took a personal role in calling for jihad and rebelling against the non-Muslim forces, from British, French, Italian and even Israeli forces. Imam Amin Al-Husseini declared a holy war and specified the task to combat the Jewish Zionist-backed State of Israel. At some point, the imam gave orders to kill and eliminate any Jew wherever he or she may be found. The Ottoman Empire was abolished in 1924 and, since then, millions of imams have called the Muslims to rebel and wage jihad and follow the example of Prophet Muhammad. Osama Bin Laden actually

After the collapse of the Ottoman caliphate

did follow Muhammad's path for the most part. The eventual aim was to establish an Islamic polity: the caliphate. The earlier mentioned Imam Al-Husseini even rallied with the Nazi Reich, hoping to stop Zionists from establishing a Jewish state in Palestine. Today, the Israeli-Palestinian dispute over the land is one of the main problematic matters within the Islamic world.

It is suitable to compare how Hitler pushed the world into World War II to how Bin Laden became a jihadist and encouraged the Muslims to wage jihad and pick up arm against the western world, which some believe will be World War III. Just like Hitler did, Bin Laden blamed the whole problems of the world on the Israel and its closest ally; the United States. Just like Hitler did with the eager Germans by enticing them against the Jews and Americans, also do most imams and preachers where they call for jihad and Islamic rebelling. Osama Bin Laden went even further than most imams and financed the militants and terrorists to accomplish their goals. In 1988, Bin Laden helped his followers to establishing the Al-Qaeda militia and provided a jihad plan that consists of several stages. The Al-Qaeda goals were to awaken the Muslims to wage an Islamic rebellion in the same manner Hitler pushed the Germans to wage the Nazi conquest.

It's also accurate to claim that Bin Laden's efforts have produced the current caliphate, the Islamic State (ISC) which he encouraged the Muslims and urged the jihadists to strive for. Osama Bin Laden's understanding of Islam affirmed that the Muslims have to be governed by an authentic Islamic regime: the caliphate. Bin Laden surely helped to revive Muhammad's prophetic project. It's all a part of Muhammad's philosophy, which promotes to form a theodemocratic socialist republic, which is more of an authoritarian empire according to many accounts.

By the 20th century

By the end of World War II, the Brits pulled out of the Middle East and left it for the regional powers to fight for. Since then, from the Zionists to the Arabic socialists, minorities and Islamic extremists; all have been conflicting over the land and its governance. All those situations and events have brought depressed and oppressed generations into the Middle East.

Since the Brits pulled out, Israel has been the most dominant power in the Middle East. That's why the second half of the 20th century became the birth point of Islamic jihadism. Since the late 1940s and after the Arab-Israeli war, the Islamic jihad campaign has increased in power and strength. In 1988, once Bin Laden and his followers formed Al-Qaeda, the modern jihadism and the current Islamic rebellion were revived and started to take place. And by today, the Islamic jihad has social, financial and political reasons as well.

The rebellious mentality

Since the Ottoman Empire's collapse in 1924, the Muslims of the Middle East have been doing whatever they can to rebuild and restore their totalitarian Islamic empire and caliphate. Osama Bin Laden was a wealthy Saudi Arabian who truly influenced the extreme Muslims and motivated them to wage the Islamic rebellion; in the same manner that Prophet Muhammad did in the 6th century.

The Arab Spring of 2011 was a major turning point for the Islamic rebellion; as the jihadists and Islamic rebels took advantage of the situation and went on to conquer vast lands, which enabled them to establish the Islamic State Caliphate in 2014.

Abraham the Patriarch's actions' inspired Muhammad. Prophet Muhammad's actions' inspired Adolf Hitler, according to some sources. Hitler's actions' inspired Michel Aflaq. Michel Aflaq's philosophy inspired the eager and striving Arabs such as Saddam Hussein and Osama Bin Laden. Osama Bin Laden inspired the Caliph Abu Bakr Al-Baghdadi, who was raised under Saddam Hussein's authority and regime. That's how the rebellious mentality has been evolved overtime, until it has reached us today in the form of Islamic jihad, war and terrorism. Today, it can be described as a religious rebellion; the Islamic rebellion.

Out of control

Middle Easterners and remnants of the Ottoman Empire are still in disarray and out of control; for the most part. Today, many mad Middle Easterners are out of control, some turn into Islamists quickly, and become jihadists who could be plotting to attack America. They try to hit America for the simple fact that they all know that the United States is the biggest financial provider to Israel. That's a point that Bin

After the collapse of the Ottoman caliphate

Laden has mentioned before, and we will discuss how the United Stated got tangled with the Arab-Israeli wars up in the next centuries.

All these events and situations have occurred after the breakdown of the Ottoman caliphate in 1924. Since then, devout and striving Arabs and Muslims have been following the Muhammadan rebellious ideology to reestablished their long-awaited dream; the Islamic caliphate. Basically, that has been the situation of the Muhammadans after the Ottoman Empire collapsed, as we're still witnessing what those extreme and devout Muhammadans are engaged in; the current Islamic rebellion.

Today, the Muhammadan rebellious mentality has become the tool and path that the Islamic rebels and jihadists tend to follow and use to accomplish their goals. Financial, emotional and social instability will increase the risk of Muslims of becoming Islamic jihadists, terrorists and rebels. Today, it's all a part of the Muhammadan swamp.

6. The truth

The Islamic rebellious ideology

The Islamic rebellious ideology is very significant for the current active empire and superpower. Today, thousands of Islamic rebels and sleeper jihadists are all over the world, in the backyards and public areas, cities, countries and continents of our planet. Muslims are learners of the Islamic rebellious philosophy at the hands of imams, who urge and call for an Islamic rebellion. Any mad and sick Muslim can become a deadly rebel at any moment, once he or she decides to become a physically active rebel.

The current superpowers are the most at risk. But this doesn't mean that people should insult, harm, or attack Muslims randomly because they follow the Islamic rebellious ideology; but to pay attention to their desires and actions, and the intentions behind them. Today, there are thousands of Islamic rebels and jihadists that are bringing havoc, so their like a needle in a haystack within the 1.7 billion Muslims.

In the 15th century, the Muslims invaded and took over Constantinople and annihilated the Eastern Roman Empire. The Muslims came suddenly, and by the time the Roman Caesar had realized the threat, it was too late. The Ottomans, led by Sultan Muhammad II, invaded and took the land and Muhammad II placed himself as the new Caesar instead of Constantine XI Palaeologus. The Roman Emperor never expected the Ottomans to attack and destroy the Byzantine Roman Empire, as the current Islamic rebellion is definitely on the same course with the current superpowers. So basically, there was an Islamic conquest since the 6th century to conquer the Roman Empire; the same way there is an Islamic conquest today to conquer what the Islamists see as their lands and belongings. Surely Osama Bin Laden played a big role in reviving the jihadi conquest.

Today, some people feel that the Islamic State Caliphate is trying to wage a war between Islam and Christianity, even though the war is between the Islamic State Caliphate and its followers against the Red Nations and their armies. But still, it's a fact that most of the current jihadists and terrorists are fighting for the sake of the Islamic liberation.

The truth

Regarding present time

On the 7th day of January 2015, the Islamic hit squad struck in Paris and accomplished their mission. They targeted the French cartoonist institution from the jihad's hit list for blaspheming Prophet Muhammad, which became known as the Charlie Hebdo attack.

Whether the hit squad was deployed by the Islamic State Caliphate or other jihadi groups isn't the case here. The bottom line is that the Islamic rebels are fighting to achieve certain goals and specific agendas. The best we can do is to stay armed and alert, until we find a peaceful solution to the Islamic rebellion and all other acts of aggression, physical conflicts, violence and war. Now, whether there will be any peace treaties or more conflicts between the Islamists and France is not the point. France should provide guidance and help to educate its Muslim populations that respect, glory, dignity, honor and victory are to be earned; not obtained by bloodshed and violence. Just like Israel, France is at high risk of the Islamic rebellion, simply because it has some of the highest Muslim populations within the Western World. More Muslims means more potential Islamic jihadists and rebels.

Respect is important for peace to be completed, as disrespect could bring hate and madness.

In general, the American people have always contributed to the world's peace, even though America is still at war with the terroristic jihadists. The Islamists and nationalist Arabs have been at war with America since the Gulf war, and still, our government interferes militarily between the Muslims and gets involved in their wars. By now we're directly included within the jihadist's wars.

Facts and claims

There is a way to fix every problem that we may face. With the knowledge and the information we have today, we should be able to contain Islamic terrorism and hopefully hang on to peace until the whole war ends and conflict comes to rest quietly.

Concerning Osama Bin Laden, he claimed that the American intervention in the Gulf War was the beginning of an occupation and then he declared war on America in return. Such events brought the destructive results that face us today, regardless of the victorious combats that we sustained in the Gulf War. The Middle East needs profound political and social reform in order for the current situation to get better—not more conflicts and wars.

The American intervention in the Gulf War to support the Saudi government against the Iraqi government caused many Muslims to be mad enough to wage war on America. America's involvements in the Gulf War fired back a decade later in 2001. During the Gulf War, President George H. Bush didn't get hurt at all but his military actions jeopardized the safety of America for a long time to come. It created lots of animosity. It proved that regardless of how successful a war campaign is, others will rebel and strike back even deadlier than imagined.

The end?

It's not the end. The year 2012 has come and the Mayan calendar was incorrect about its prediction of our demise.

Since World War I, many African nations have struggled with the British, French and Italian colonial misuse and abuse of the continent. Mentioning so will not help the African people, but it's a reminder of what colonizing and imperialism creates. The European colonization was the end for Africa, where until this day, many African nations are still struggling politically. In Africa, many children are still experiencing turmoil, and in some areas on daily basis. A decent life in those parts of the world ended a long time ago, and some Africans feel as if they are living in hell since then.

Even in India, millions are still suffering since the Brits occupied that nation during the past few centuries. Today, India has millions of people who live in slums and have almost no way out. Even the Middle East was affected by British colonization. The people of the Middle East were doing okay until the British government went over and beat down the Ottoman rule and occupied their lands. The Brits sent Lawrence of Arabia—he was like James Bond—who led the area straight to sedition and conflict instead of helping them to become better people and gain a prosperous future.

Review and examine how the British rule over the Middle East paved the way for Saddam Hussein to come to power. Saddam Hussein ruling Iraq was the cause of the 2003 war that President George W. Bush initiated. If Saddam Hussein was not there in the first place, President Bush would've never had the opportunity or the reason to send our men and women to that war. The long-term effects of the British rule in Iraq become disastrous in latter times.

Animosity

The American invasion of Iraq caused millions of Arabs and Muslims to develop a grudge toward the American leadership and its supporters. But still, do not stop supporting the American government just because there is someone who despises it or because some politicians are abusing their power. Better yet, choose the right leaders to govern us by voting and making sure they stay on a righteous path.

Lots of Arabs love America, but surely the orphans of the American invasion of Iraq will have some hate and animosity against America. Bin Laden dragged the Arabs into this war, and President George W. Bush's administration took the bait and invaded Iraq. Obviously, Saddam Hussein was unable to protect his land from the invasion that caused instability, which divided Iraq and brought a worse future on the region. That's why many Iraqi orphans became jihadists to rebel as some joined the Islamic State Caliphate ranks already.

But that Islamic-American animosity was there long before the 2003 invasion, one might say. That is true. As a matter of a fact, the 2003 invasion of Iraq was a result of Islamists attacking America on September 11, 2001. But still, the American causalities in Iraq and Afghanistan proved to the rest that America is not untouchable. Also, America is a sensitive country with a very conscious population, as we saw after the 9/11 attacks. The Americans didn't call for war; it was President George W. Bush who invaded Iraq with the 192,000 man force.

Pressure points of jihad

After the invasion of Iraq, young Arab patriots, and avid Muslims turned to resist the invasion and responded to the jihad calls of their imam Osama Bin Laden. That's what diverted the Al-Qaeda troops to Iraq under the appointed jihadi warrior, Abu Musab Al-Zarqawi.

Why do some Muslims hate America?

Regardless of the old problems, the invasion of Iraq created more hatred by many Muslims on America. Muslims turn into Islamists in a heartbeat when it comes to dedicating their money, bodies and souls for the sake of the Islamic liberation. Some rebel against the opposition and tend not to sit around watching their fellow jihadists get beat and

The truth

lose. The jihad front has become stronger since Bin Laden formed the global jihadi squad to conquer the Islamic lands. They conquered Afghanistan from the USSR all right, but then they were looking at the other Muslim homelands; while they're eyes have always been on what they call Palestine. Bin Laden urged the Muslims to give it their all and form a united structure to bring glory back to Islam and Muslims. The 2003 Iraq invasion increased the Muslims' response to his calls, especially the young ones, who had developed high emotional differentiation after the wrongful invasion. Osama Bin Laden urged the Muslims to reunite under one banner, and that's why *Muhammad's black banner of war* was brought back by the Iraqi jihadists council (MSC) while Al-Zarqawi established the jihading structure from '03-'06.

Before Bin Laden came to the scene, the jihadists were spread throughout the world. Then, he formed the jihad structure to lead the global jihad alliance in 1988, known as Al-Qaeda, which went on to operate from Afghanistan. From that point, Al-Qaeda led the alliance of the global jihadi fronts into the unification of one organization. The unity increased the power of the militant factions of the jihad, which caused some to control certain provinces and townships, as the Taliban controlling Afghanistan, Hamas controlling southwest Israel – Gaza strip, and Abu Sayyaf militia in the Philippines, etc. Those are just a few examples of Islamic jihadists and rebel groups that came to power during the end of the 20th century. The primary cause was to gain an Islamic liberation from any unwanted powers, enforce sharia laws, apply Islamic socialism, and govern the Muslims through an Islamic caliphate just like before the Ottoman Empire collapsed in the 1920s. The Islamic law is a socialist conservative model of social justice, where everyone is to be treated equally. That's why the extreme and poor Muslims rebel; they're in need of social justice and they claim that no one will provide it like Muhammad offered it in his political system and theological polity.

After the 2003 Iraq invasion

After seven years of the American occupation of Iraq from '04-'11, thousands of American soldiers lost their lives, trillions of dollars were wasted, and years of instability were brought to Iraq. America is still vulnerable to attacks by the jihadi fronts, easier than before since the jihad movement gained numbers and strength afterward. Al-Qaeda was able to hold firm in Iraq until Al-Zarqawi was killed. Bin Laden was still enjoying the news of Americans dying in the Sunni Triangle in Iraq. He must've felt that it was like the Bermuda Triangle that he dragged America into. Soon enough, the American economy was falling apart and by 2008, the recession came about, which was a major blow to the America, which must've flattered Bin Laden. Let's keep in mind that Bin Laden's number one goal of his jihad was to destroy America, mainly by hitting its economy, and that's why they struck the world trade center.

As President Barack Obama took office, all the American troops were pulled out of Iraq, and the country was handed to a newly formed Shia government. That enabled Al-Qaeda to take advantage of the new weak government of Iraq after President Obama pulled out the American troops in 2011.

Al-Qaeda in Iraq along the Monotheism and Jihad Group (JTJ) and other Sunni militant and jihadi groups, formed the jihadists counsel (MSC) in Iraq in 2004 and had three different leaders and successors by 2010. The jihadists counsel (MSC) formed a government and rebelled against the new Iraqi government after the Arab Spring. The current caliphate (ISC) was established in 2014, despite the fact that Bin Laden was killed in action three years before that. Matter of a fact, Bin Laden had addressed that jihad would continue whether he was around or not, and so the Islamic rebellion goes.

By 2014, the Islamic State Caliphate was recruiting tens of thousands of followers and was able to conquer northern Iraq and even annex eastern Syria. Soon enough, the Islamic State Caliphate captured more than ten cities and started performing Quranic governance in its territories. Finally, in some sense, after twenty-five years, Bin Laden's efforts became very fruitful, which resulted in the reinitiating and reestablishment of the Islamic caliphate. The Islamic State Caliphate abolished the border between Iraq and Syria and gave its citizens the right to enjoy moving around the land without any national barriers.

Future jihadists

Keep in mind that all children are being raised at the moment and they're forming their personal and social foundations. Millions of kids in Africa suffer, as children are the most vulnerable individuals out of the whole world's population. Some Iraqi sources claim that there are

The truth

over three million orphans in Iraq alone as a result of the 2003 American invasion.

Today, the Islamic State Caliphate is recruiting hundreds; if not thousands of young men to become the next wave of Islamic militants and terrorists. Not just the ISC, many jihadi groups are doing so as well.

That's how the Islamists' strategy has worked and the American foreign policy has failed. "The big whale took the bait," Al-Baghdadi I said in one of his speeches. It's a part of their psychological war. Most of the current Islamic rebels are young Muslims that feed on jihadi propaganda. How come older Muslims don't commit suicide jihad? The answer predicts what the future may look like.

If humanity does not reach the roots of the matter as a whole, then the future that awaits us will be very problematic. Children will keep having the same problems, and the same old thing will regrow back and could even get worse. Apparently, not all neglected Muslim children and orphans fall victims to such cracks in humanity. But many children, in general, are being misused and abused by many societies. Something needs to be done to change the whole transgression issue. President Obama's changes in the Middle East caused more problems than solving.

It's our duty to correct the young children's traits and teach them the right way to live while they're young; they're minds are growing, and their personalities are developing. By the time they reach maturity and the stage of reason and action, it will be natural for them to live clean, upright, and honorable lives. That's the only way to kill the snake. That's the best way to eliminate aggression and mischief at the source before it consumes all of us, as it will save the children from falling in that path. The main causes of mischief are the improper teaching, lack of knowledge, and hostile environments. Millions of kids around the world are falling behind, so within the next years and decades, billions could go astray. The symptom must be diagnosed in order for the next generations to improve by teaching their children instead of having future generations fight each other. It's humanity's duty and should be worked on now instead of waiting until it's too late. The whole Muslim and non-Muslim world should work on this issue.

Wars never solve problems permanently

Acts of war such as the 2003 invasion of Iraq caused thousands

The truth

of provoked and bloodthirsty Muslims to find another reason to rebel and wage Islamic terror. For example, Al-Zarqawi took advantage of America's mistake, as he brought thousands of jihadists along to fight and combat the American troops in that part of the world. Today, his old friends and fellow jihadists made up ISI and ISIS which became ISC.

On September 11th, 2001, America was attacked, but Iraq had nothing to do with those attacks at all. But when President Bush sent our American troops to invade Iraq for his imaginary WMDs, Al-Qaeda loved it for the mere fact that they were able to benefit from removing Saddam Hussein from the scene. But for President George W. Bush, it was "a crusade" that "is going to take a while" as he said in 2001, to defeat "Gog and Magog...in the Middle East", as he told the French President Jacques Chirac in a 2003 telephone call. Under President George W. Bush, America failed twice. Once by not protecting itself from the terrorist attacks and secondly by attacking and invading other nations; Iraq and Afghanistan, which both failed at locating or stopping Bin Laden. So it's accurate to mark the '03 Iraq invasion as a total failure.

The 2003 invasion gave the Middle Easterners more reasons to rebel against America, as the news of the war was broadcaster all over the world. It was visible to the Arabs and Muslims on TV; certain channels were dedicated all day to providing a truthful reality to the resistance that the jihadists were conducting in Iraq. While the American troops were getting caught by IED's in Iraq, there were special TV channels that showed how the resistance was going. They aired 24/7 commercial-free, showing American troops getting shot, blown up and killed. Millions of young Arabs and Muslims were watching those channels only to be incited to be fearless and commit jihad and holy war against America.

That media coverage of the American troops getting attacked in Iraq is bearing fruit; and that's why we see thousands of Muslims have been coming out to fighting America as well. Such coverage became a learning center for desperate, sick and mad Muslims to learn to attack their opponents without any hesitation. The jihad propaganda entices the lost souls to become bloodthirsty jihadists, and go on to rebel at some point in the far future. It really plays a big part and reaches their emotional instability and encourages them to follow the jihadists lead.

What needs to be understood is that Islamic rebels are aiming to

The truth

break the American superpower in order for Islam to produce the next superpower. The Muslim youth is steady being taught about the events and reminded by the imams on how the jihad should go. This phenomenon occurred since the Gulf War, but it has increased since the 2000s, after the American armed forces entered Iraq and Afghanistan, where young Muslims seen and learned of the wars destructive side. The American invasions gave Al-Qaeda more evidence to back up their claims about the American imperialism. Today, many Saudi youth view Bin Laden as a hero, a martyr and an idol. Millions of Muslim youth are being raised to wage the next war on America, which could occur by the 2030s-2050, if left unchecked. Saudi Arabia, in particular, has the most jihad loving youth out of the entire Muslim world due to the Islamic extremism within the country. The more Arab tyrannies are ignored throughout the Middle East, the more risks will come in place. The CIA can't solve it alone; neither can the US Army. It must be solved from the inside out. In this case, we have to go after the corrupted Muslim leaders and manage to fix the problems their creating. Diplomacy and fair political procedures, along with education will solve the problem.

Few thoughts

For now, there must be millions of Muslim children at risk of becoming the next armed rebels and militants, ready to blow objects up and take others with them in order to gain their ideal Islamic liberation. It's up to us whether this phenomenon continues to take place and drag humanity down or straighten this matter and bring total peace back instead of increasing the bloody scenes.

We're in the make-it-or-break-it stage. We're facing the fact that Armageddon has started and we need to find a way to solve this problem. Consider Abu Bakr Al-Baghdadi. From his side, he's a man who probably has seen the worst of it. He was detained and spent time locked up during the Iraq war. According to him, some outside armies came and invaded his country back in '03 when he was still an average civilian who then got held up and lost his freedom for a while. He probably was troubled by the experience and maybe his family as well. The problem is that these people feel that there's a war on Muslims, and some of the politicians in our leadership try to act like if there's nothing going on. Not all Arabs are Muslims, but it's Arab Muslims who are

The truth

waging the war. The truth is there's a war between some western powers and their opposition. The extreme Muslims, imams, and Islamologists are waging jihad and holy war on what they call *crusaders and Zionists*. It's the war versus the Islamic rebellion. By now, other younger Muslims might become radicalized and continue the war on Israel and America. Those then will attract and recruit more brainwashed kids, who are simply social rebels, to join the Islamic rebellion and raise more jihad. Today, even the disfranchised Baathists in Iraq are joining the jihadists for the simple fact that that they provide them with jobs and income.

It's understandable to any conscious American that if our country goes to a full-scale war with the Islamic State Caliphate, it will be a hideous one. America is on the very edge of bankrupting, and one more Middle Eastern war will bring the second great depression about, and that will result in millions of more Americans falling in poverty. The war between the Zionists and the jihadists is spilling into both, the Muslim and the Western world, and we have to find a peaceful solution as soon as possible. If the conflict is accumulating on people who don't do anything, then we all have to do something to combat it before it's too late. It's a very sensitive matter, and that's why we provided this warning.

Be aware

This warning is a clear statement and an urgent call to step to the safe side. We must comprehend that World War III that started at 8:48 a.m. eastern time, on the morning of September 11, 2001, out of New York City.

The world seemed to have lived in denial before the 9/11 attacks. During those years before the 9/11 attacks, the Islamic rebellion was barely improving and gaining a momentum that dragged the United States of America into chaos, along with many other people and governments who were also indirectly affected. The Islamic terrorism and jihadism increased the volume of unrest and instability that was witnessed after the 9/11 attacks. Even Saudi Arabia, Afghanistan, England, France, Canada, Iraq, Syria, Libya, Yemen, Somalia, Pakistan, Lebanon, Jordan, Turkey and NATO were affected by the 9/11 attacks.

The Islamic rebellion also indirectly brought some destruction to Kenya, Tanzania and Nigeria. It affected the world's economy and opened up a vital page in the history of the religious apocalypses. The

The truth

Islamic rebels and terrorists are on the slaying mode, for now. The war with the Islamists changed our lives into a situation of wars and new realities to deal with. We must stay aware about that.

Ugly truths

Every person needs peace, but for the sick, mad and violent Muslims, peace is not on their wish list. Today, the Islamic jihadism is flooding the world because of the amount of the mistreated children. There have been some warriors, like Genghis Khan and Adolf Hitler, who grew up to engage their people in massive warfare because they were abused when they were children. Even Saddam Hussein, Prophet Muhammad and many other mighty men, have had harsh childhoods. They all dealt with their tarnished societies by using their political knowledge and capabilities, as they grew older and became army leaders.

Though President George W. Bush had a decent childhood and education, he invaded Iraq; a nation that had no threat to the United States of America nor played any role in the 9/11 attacks. May he did rely on his understanding of some biblical prophecies to initiate the war, but invading Iraq without a probable cause was unjustifiable realistically. Unjustifiable wars are an ugly truth that we must face and deal with wisely, instead of committing more which would fire back eventually.

45th and 46th Presidents' duty

Clearly, many people started to feel that President Obama started looking like President George W. Bush regarding the foreign policy failure while in office. If the 43rd and 44th Presidents failed with combating Islamic terrorism, we need the next two presidents to turn the tides around and bring the 80's and 90s' glory back. We need to bring the American soldiers back home and leave the Old World alone. Germany, Jordan, or Japan don't need the American troops; our soldiers could be securing our borders instead of protecting other nations.

For the 2016 elections, if Mrs. Hillary Clinton gets elected, she will also be a failure if she doesn't bring the American troops home and save our money. Mr. Donald Trump seems very interested in saving America and interested less in shedding blood. Even though he seems to tell the truth, the whole truth and nothing but the truth, many Americans still do not understand him due to some of the media's depiction and misrepresentation of his desires, along with his gruff and harsh tone and words. Other than that gentleman, most other republicans seem out of context regarding finding solutions to the Islamic jihading, rebelling and terrorism problems.

Interfering with the Islamic world brings lots of problems to us and may also cost more lives and billions of dollars. Regardless, fixing our domestic problems is more important, and our 45th and 46th presidents should be interested in that rather than policing the world and interfering with the problems of other nations. Shedding blood and putting American lives at risk, as President George W. Bush did during his war campaigns, is never a healthy thing at all.

Wounded American

Let's go back and recount the American lives lost in previous wars and speculate about the future numbers of wounded warriors and soldiers. The Vietnam War left about 58,000 American soldiers killed and 300,000 wounded. Going back to World War II, we had up to 290,000 American soldiers killed and around 670,000 soldiers hurt. Fast forward to the 2003 invasion of Iraq, it took the lives of about 4,400 American soldiers and injured around 32,000. The Iraq war affected and hurt more than 36,000 Americans in total, other than their families.

Since the Islamic State Caliphate has gained momentum and strength, we can predict that the next Middle East war may result in many times as much the damage as the '03 war. According to what we have seen already and by the way the Islamic State Caliphate is increasing in numbers and power, we can speculate that the next war in the Middle East might result in the injury of tens, if not hundreds, of thousands of military personnel, wounded; either fatally or not.

Just as explained in century 4, we're better off staying out of the Muhammadan swamp. That's why the 45th and 46th presidents have the most crucial duties regarding the Islamic rebellion. We have explained how Muhammad's invention of jihad caused his Muslim community to gain power to end up breaking the Roman Empire. So we must be careful with warring with such violent and mad Muslims because we're seeing how far they will take it, as suicide and terror attacks have become their fad. We need to stay safe and out of harms' way and combat violence with common sense. These are the ugliest truths that we have to be aware of regarding the current Islamic rebellion, as it goes on.

7. Here we are

Civil society dilemmas

If there's an outlaw in the area, such as a robber who finds comfort in stealing, then the civilians need to be cautious and aware of their surroundings and the risks of their environment. It's the same potential dilemma that correctional officers and prison guards face and live with every time they're on the job.

In 2015 and on a train in Europe, three American military servicemen thwarted a terrorist attack by stopping, restraining and overcoming the assailant. The offender was armed with a machine gun. Their attention and swift actions is what prevented the attack.

When the population and the people inhabit a tight and a close-linked area such as cities, the risk of such harm and volume of damage grows much higher than the populations in the countryside or desolate lands face. So, the masses in populated cities are at much greater risk of criminals than those of the country and desolate areas.

Terrifying attacks of Islamic terrorists such as the ones in London, Baghdad, New York City, Paris and Ben Ghazi, which witnessed firsthand destruction through physical attacks of jihadists, should be kept in mind and taken as a lesson to learn from. This warning goes to every single person who resides in the rest of the cities that contain millions of people at any given moment. All the potential endangered people should be warned and become cautious of the applicable devastation that could hit any city or urban area of this world.

Pick an option

Do not stress out; instead, every city resident should recognize his or her personal responsibility to cope with our current global problems.

You, the reader, may not have too many excellent options if you fail to protect yourself after receiving this warning. At any given moment, each adult carries the responsibilities of preserving his/her safety, protecting his/her life, and caring for his/her personal peace and comfort.

Fox news commentator Mr. Bill O'Reilly has stated that "we should get the world to rally" against violence and terrorism, and the people should actually do more concerning this matter. But how can we do so if most Muslims are alienated from our civilization as they live in desolate areas of the Old World such as Africa and South Asia? Maybe capable Muslims and their governments should be doing so.

If we have coped with such realities and our government is dealing with the issue, why can't others, such as the Arab and Muslim leaders, get involved with solving this issue peacefully with proper actions? Their negligence is what leaves the rest with very few options, so we're better off holding and maintaining peace within our nation. In the next quatrains, we will go through some suggestions on how to deal with this matter, under the quatrain "Advice, cautions, warnings."

Sheikh – Head of jihadists, and Caliph – Islamic nation prince

In the current stage of the Islamic rebellion, Bin Laden came at a sensitive time; he led the jihad and rebelling movement at various levels in order to gain an Islamic liberation. At first, the jihad's uprising focused on targets in the Middle East and the Arabian Peninsula region such as the USS Cole and Khobar Towers bombings. Bin Laden was born into a billionaire Saudi family that thrived in the modern construction business by building projects. Instead, he invested into the making of the jihadi group formation; Al-Qaeda, which was preparing of war to engage in combat operations in the Islamic world. Bin Laden financed the jihad front, whose primary cause was to regain control of the Holy Lands and obtain an Islamic liberation. Undoubtedly Jerusalem is included, as Mecca and Yathrib (Medina) are also on their list. It's supposed to be a repeat to what Muhammad did, where the 6th caliphate's conquest reached as far east as China and as far west as Spain.

Once the former Ottoman caliphate was officially abolished by Turkey's nationalists in the 1920s, the Caliph Sultan Abdul Majid was exiled, the Islamic caliphate was dismantled and Turkey was transformed into a new secular nation. The Ottomans left the remnants of the caliphate behind to fend for themselves and survive on their own. The last Sultan Abdul Majid, who was exiled, was also the last Emir Al-Mumineen (Islamic nation prince) of the Ottoman Dynasty.

Even though Bin Laden did not earn the title of caliph, he was given the title Sheikh Al Mujahedeen, which means *the head of striving Muslims*. He was elected as the leader of the Islamic jihad movement that later became known as Al-Qaeda. Their first goal was rid of the Middle Eastern regimes. The second goal of the Islamic rebellion, as we know, is to restore the caliphate. Let's make it clear: Al-Qaeda is the jihadi movement that's supposed to be rebelling against the secular governments throughout the Islamic world, while the caliphate is a governmental structure and body of an Islamic political statehood. That's why the current caliphate is called the Islamic State Caliphate and is a political municipality; not only a jihad group. If Bin Laden were here today, he probably would've advised the Muslims to go to the Islamic State and support the caliphate, since that was his greater goal. He always urged the Muslims to reestablish a Quranic Muhammadan caliphate.

During the progress and advancement of the Islamic rebellion, the caliphate was restored as Al-Baghdadi II picked up the duty and confirmed the goal which is to liberate all the Islamic lands and unite them with the rest of the Islamic States Caliphate.

The revival of jihad

Bin Laden took a personal role in the revival of the quest to conquer the Islamic world as he tried to bring the Muslims back into one united Islamic nation. Obviously, the jihad's progression is still in effect, as thousands of admirers are volunteering to continue the mission. It took decades in order for the Islamic rebellion to reach the position that it has advanced to by today. The issue affects the world, our economy, our stability, and the security of the Red Nations specifically.

They want to be like Moses, they say

Let's mention another ideology that jihadists follow, to understand how they think. Let's also keep in mind that many Islamists have been striving in the mission to wage a holy war. The best example is Osama Bin Laden and his type of Islamists and their rebellion. They claim that they strive for God's sake. Muslims also consider the Egyptian Prophet, Moses, to have been a jihadi as he rebelled against the Pharaoh; for God's sake. Regardless of what they claim, we can recognize that Moses was a religious rebel and the jihadists are trying to copy him.

One revolution at a time

The evolution of the Islamic rebellion goes on. Billions of people struggle with the philosophy that came out of the Judeo-Christian prophecies, which Muhammad adapted and reformed into the religious ideology of Islam. He produced a theological state by combining Islam with the social justice model of direct democracy that Plato presented.

Today, we come to find the fingers pointed at the current extreme Muslims and Islamists who want to bring the Muhammadan caliphate back by any means; even by force. They follow the Quran as their constitution and the Sharia Law as their legislation. The Quran is totally anti-evangelical, as the Muhammadan Islamic philosophy totally criticizes, contradicts and conflicts with the Holy Bible head on, and the belief of the Holy Trinity and the crucifixion of Jesus Christ.

Uglier truths

Not just the United Stated, even the Netherlands, France, Australia, Belgium, Denmark and Britain experienced the jihadists and rebels' terror as well. The rest of the Red Nations are being warned about the consequences of engaging in conflicts with the Islamic rebellion or the jihadists. It is an ugly reality, but we must confront it head on in order for us to solve the problem. Today, here we are at war with them.

Citizens, governments, and leaders of the Red Nations should recalculate their steps and rethink their actions. If people were misled and misguided to join the conflict, then they must pull out and keep a distance from such headaches. Otherwise, more interference might get the Red Nations sucked down the Muhammadan swamp. If not, a full scare war should take place as soon as possible before the ISC gets too powerful. It's one of the ugliest truths that we're facing during our era.

Socialist Islamic republic

Though some significant jihadi figures were advanced, educated, and modernized civilians who became radicalized with time, let's keep in mind that most Islamists come from poor and uncivilized backgrounds. As it is classified, the current Islamic rebellion has a lot to do with the lack of social justice within the Islamic world. So they're in pursuit of an Islamic liberation from secularity, nationalism, liberalism, capitalism, atheism and communism. Islamists want a socialist Islamic republic to be governed by Muhammad's Sharia Law. It is meant to subject every Muslim into a one supreme configuration, according to the Muhammadan Islamic caliphate regime. That's what the Islamic rebellion is all about; building a global caliphate that cares for all and every Muslim and eliminate mankind's struggle.

Here we are

Picking sides?

Today, it's just like what President George W. Bush said, "you're either with us, or against us." So we must speak out loudly, where staying silent is a part of accepting the mischief by leaving it to thrive. Picking sides is an important issue, and choosing the right side is the best way to go when dealing with such intense matters. For example, the Islamic State Caliphate is encouraging Muslims to join the caliphate and support their jihadi campaign. How come we do not see the western powers checking and evaluating who's on our side and who's not? Well, maybe they're ignoring this matter, and that's why we warn about the carelessness of the situation.

The Islamic State of Iraq (ISI)

Upon the decisions of President George W. Bush and his orders to invade Iraq in 2003, the former Iraqi president Saddam Hussein was removed from office, which left Iraq in total disarray as its governance became a free for all. In 2004, the Al-Qaeda jihadist Al-Zarqawi intervened and led an Islamic resistance against the American forces. He and several Sunni jihadist groups made up a jihadi consultation council, better known as MSC. Al-Zarqawi was promoted to a general, as his troops were able to hold the Sunni Triangle for three years until he was killed in 2006. Soon after, the jihadists' council (MSC) secretly elected a new head for their governing body of the Islamic State of Iraq, who called himself Abu Omar Al-Baghdadi (Al-Baghdadi I, shown on the back cover), who also died in action in 2010. But in 2006, after Al-Zarqawi's death, they secretly formed the Islamic State of Iraq (ISI). The Islamic State of Iraq was not disclosed to the public until it annexed eastern Syria under the leadership of Al-Baghdadi II in 2014. The Islamic State of Iraq added *Syria* to the name, so it became the Islamic State of Iraq and Syria: ISIS. Upon that event, the jihadists' council (MSC) approved Al-Baghdadi II to be a caliph, and thus the Islamic caliphate was revived in June 2014. That's how ISI of October 2006 became ISIS in 2014, which finally enabled the Quranic caliphate to come back to life.

As President George W. Bush took out Saddam Hussein's regime, the Islamic State of Iraq was formed and led by jihadists after the approval of the jihadists' council (MSC) in October, 2006. President George W. Bush failed at his job for protecting America and instead, he destroyed Iraq. He claimed that he invaded Iraq to free the Iraqi people, but it seems that the Iraqi people didn't benefit as much as those who benefitted from the removal of Saddam Hussein, such as Iran and the jihadists who took advantage of the situations since then. But obviously, he ordered the invasion to defeat "Gog and Magog…in the Middle East", as he told the French President Jacques Chirac in the 2003 phone call.

Islamic State of Iraq and Syria (ISIS) – a step closer to Armageddon?

An Islamic caliphate can be seen today in the Islamic State Caliphate in Iraq and Syria. It was formed in 2014 by the jihadists of Syria and ISI, which automatically placed it in the United Nations terrorist list. In return, President Obama automatically formed the Red Nations coalition to engage in the anti-Islamic State campaign.

The Arab spring that President Obama stood behind opened the door for the jihadists to gain vast control and govern the lands they conquered in the Middle East. The jihadists were able to form a Quranic judicial system for an Islamic caliphate, which helped the uniting of the Islamic State in Iraq and Syria. Thousands of Islamists in Yemen, Afghanistan, Egypt, Nigeria, Somalia and Libya have joined along and pledged allegiance to the caliph Al-Baghdadi II. The Islamic State's capital is Al-Raqqah, and Abu Bakr Al-Baghdadi became the first caliph to exist since Abdul Majid of the Ottoman Empire was removed in 1924.

In February 2015, President Obama affirmed that the 2003 Iraq invasion opened the door for the Islamic rebellion to gain a foothold in the Middle East. He called it an unintentional consequence. Let's not forget how President Obama supported arming some Syrians to rebel and wage war, such as the Free Syrian Army; which also was a major mistake. The Syrian rebels turned out to be extreme Islamists and jihadists. They were being called freedom fighters while they were terroristic jihadists who were building a Quranic caliphate. And then, they called war on the Red Nations once they were combated.

Many Red Nations are getting hit as well. Japan, England, Poland, Jordan, Spain, Egypt, France and many more countries have brought death upon their civilians by fighting the ISC since 8/8/2014. Let's suppose that the 9/11 attacks took place and additional major attacks were repelled; the August 8th, 2014 Air Strike campaign ordered by President Obama opened a new wave of death upon the Red Nations.

Here we are

It is time to realize, if no one has noticed yet. When we fight a war with people who fly jumbo jets into buildings and wear suicide belts to avenge, then it's time to wake up and realize that this war doesn't and will not stop with simply winning one or two battles. But we believe that it's the final phase of the Islamic rebellion, which as mentioned earlier, might lead to World War III and put us to the test with the great battle of Armageddon. Here we are. We have the Islamic State Caliphate (ISC) that's fighting till death, and we have the Red Nations coalition that is at war with it, as the civilians are the scapegoats of the politicians' actions.

The Red Nations vs. Islamic State Caliphate

On August 8, 2014 President Obama ordered air strikes and military operations against the Islamic State Caliphate. It was a part of his anti-Islamic State campaign, where he invited more than 60 nations to take a part in the war against the rebellious Islamic State Caliphate. These 60+ volunteering countries came to be named the Red Nations since the Islamic State Caliphate vowed to soak those nations in blood at every possible chance. Many nations became involved in the war against the Islamic State Caliphate, which came in place as a result of the Islamic rebellion's accomplishments. We call those countries the Red Nations.

If the United States of America, United Kingdom, Spain, Norway, Denmark, Canada, Belgium, Australia, Ukraine, China, Switzerland, Serbia, Montenegro, Moldova, Macedonia, Kosovo, Korea, Japan, Georgia, Oman, Kuwait, Bosnia, Cyprus, Sweden, Finland, Austria, Slovenia, Slovakia, Romania, Lithuania, Latvia, Ireland, Israel, Iceland, Czech, Poland, Hungary, Greece, Estonia, Croatia, Bulgaria, Albania, Tunisia, Somalia, Qatar, Saudi Arabia, Turkey, Portugal, Jordan, Russia, Bahrain, Morocco, Iraq, Lebanon, Libya, and Egypt are at war with the current Islamic State Caliphate, then they must be careful with their next actions. We warn because the Islamic State Caliphate has sleeper cells, jihadists and terrorists all throughout the land. The current Afrasian migration to Europe is another way of infiltration by the Islamic State Caliphate and other supporters of the Islamic rebellion. Some sleeper cells even have combat training and are capable of jihading and fighting wherever they're placed. They might come in waves of terror. Provoking them may bring havoc and cause disturbance of peace, obliteration, and physical destruction to the livelihoods of the citizens of the Red Nations. As long as the jihad calls continue throughout the world, we might have some Islamists and sympathizers, and maybe even some sleeper rebels who are not active yet, attack suddenly. It is a fact that the Islamic State Caliphate did not directly target the United States until the Red Nations coalition was formed by President Obama and engaged with the air strikes campaign. The Islamic State Caliphate was left with few options, and surely the dedicated jihadists weren't simply going to give up. Declaring war on the Red Nations was formally announced by the Islamic State Caliphate right away, and that's when the caliphate began executing Americans in return. James Foley was the first American victim from the Red Nations.

Underground Terrorist Group (UTG)

The reality is whether the group was called the jihadists council (MSC), Al-Qaeda in Iraq (AQI), the Islamic State of Iraq (ISI), the Islamic State of Iraq and Syria (ISIS) or the Islamic State Caliphate (ISC) it's actually the same group of jihadists and Islamic fighters who have pledged allegiance to Al-Zarqawi under the discretion of Osama Bin Laden back in 2004. From Al-Zarqawi until Al-Baghdadi II, the jihadist group has been following the same agendas provided by Al-Qaeda.

The group has been studied by the American intelligence and investigation agencies since the beginning. The first militant group was established in 2003 as the American troops entered Iraq. At first it was called the Monotheism and Jihad Group (JTJ). It was formed by the fallen Iraqi army officers along with local Sunni fighters and other foreign jihadists. The resistance group received many foreign fighters at the time, and Al-Zarqawi was one of them, who moved from Jordan to Iraq in 2004. Al-Zarqawi traveled to Iraq to wage war on the Americans on behalf of Osama Bin Laden, as Al-Zarqawi knew Bin Laden in person. The jihadists' council (MSC) was formed between Al-Zarqawi's Al-Qaeda group in Iraq and the Monotheism and Jihad Group (JTJ), where Al-Zarqawi was elected to be the leader because he was supported and trained by Al-Qaeda during the 1990's. Before Al-Zarqawi died, he urged his followers to establish the Islamic State of Iraq, which they did a few months after his death. The same jihadi group went by the name of Monotheism and Jihad Group (JTJ) but subsequently changed the name to the Islamic State of Iraq (ISI), which became the Islamic State of Iraq

Here we are

and Syria (ISIS) in 2014 after eastern Syria was annexed to ISI.

After the death of Al-Zarqawi in 2006, and by the orders of Al-Baghdadi I, the jihading project was kept concealed and went underground until the group took advantage of the Arab Spring, which enabled the Islamic State of Iraq to become the Islamic State of Iraq and Syria (ISIS), which allowed the establishment of the current caliphate (ISC) under the leadership of Al-Baghdadi II. While this was occurring, the American intelligence services were recording the movements' actions and treating them as an Underground Terrorist Group (UTG). In the diagram below, the evolution of the group that resulted in the initiation of the current caliphate can be seen along with the leaders and dates.

Basically, Al-Qaeda's involvement in the Iraq war has paved the way for the caliphate to be revived. The Arab Spring civil wars helped the jihadists gain power and territory. The warriors, rebels, and jihadists mostly formed a bunch of Underground Terrorist Groups (UTGs) until they declared the revival of the Muhammadan Quranic caliphate in 2014, and then they were combatted by the Red Nations. Before the Islamic State Caliphate was announced, the world deemed such Islamic groups as UTGs, and once the jihadists reestablished the caliphate, it became a PTG: a publicized terrorist group.

Today, after decades of the war on terror, the Islamic State Caliphate is the most publicized terrorist group worldwide. It's also the most infamous caliphate ever to exist. This reality became more obvious when the ISC announced that it consists of the Islamic jihading army that would wage the battle of Armageddon of the end times. Obviously that army will also be regarded as a UTG until it reaches the lands of Israel and fights the final battle. But today, the Islamic State Caliphate (ISC) claims that it has paved the way for the white horse rider of the apocalypses, which is mentioned in the Bible's revelations.

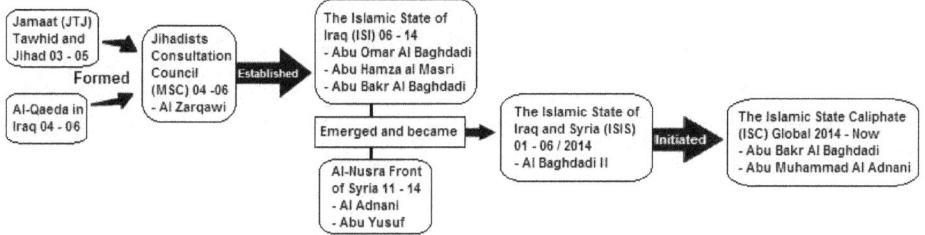

79

8. UNITE! And peace, or World War III

Global tensions

Has anyone checked out the Turkish and Israeli leaders' war of words?

What is taking place is global sedition, as some world leaders keep adding fuel to the fire. The sedition, as mentioned, has affected many cities globally. Many residents of the world's cities are looking for logical answers, so here's what the rotation in our modern cities is like:

Concerning your city

Every city in the world goes through rough times. In the past, many cities were utterly devastated by chaos and instability. If illicit drugs are a problem in society, just like uncontrollable diseases, the Islamic rebellion is just one more issue on the list for the international community to fix. It needs to be solved positively and fixed permanently, especially in the affected areas of the Islamic world that keeps the problem going.

All cities in our civilization can potentially fall victim to such rough times. Regardless of how powerful nations and their governments are, the Red Nations' cities face a larger threat from the Islamic rebellion than other countries.

New material needs to be taught to the newer generations. Updating the curriculum regarding the international community's future, to counteract the current ignorance, is essential to building a better society of the future. Today's education teaches obedience, not success. The jihadists are very aware of the insecurity and crisis in the western world; they have and do their own education and research.

It's up to the people, depending on how much they care about their children's future to react on time or just let it consume their descendants down the road. The point is that a global revolution was triggered by the jihadists a few decades ago, and by now it has expanded, gained more supporters, and is affecting more cities around the world. If you reside in the Red Nations, your city might be affected as well.

Millions of people are under the effect of this problem as many cities raise worse generations by neglecting the youth. Here's the proof. In America, most criminals come from the city. So whether it's good versus evil, right versus wrong, strong versus weak, or rich versus poor, cities face more threats, as the Islamic rebellion is just one out of many.

Global cooperation between the Abrahamic faiths and their followers is the one and only way to eliminate the aggression and violent conflicts from the Middle East. All were caused because of human errors, so keep in mind that only righteous people can solve it. The children are the most vulnerable victims in this matter.

Political conflicts got us here, and in some places around the world, survival is only for the strongest. That's why criminals and savages are rising in numbers and gaining power. Most current politicians are sticking to ignorance concerning needy people, who are left behind to fall into the cracks of the system as the rest of the world moves on. Today, the savage and barbarian packs are catching up and some are beating the wise and educated masses.

In and out of the city

In the city, people survive by their hard work while the governments uphold the law to keeps the order. For the most part, produce, utilities and services are shared by all people, as the goods are brought in via importers and traders.

On the other hand, the rest of the populations outside of the cities are living in less privileged communities. They're in a constant human struggle and are not well provided by medical, communication and transportation services. Poor people of rural areas miss much more necessities to enjoy comfortable lives than the urban residents.

Islam because of poverty

Sixth century Islam thrived by gaining support of the poor and weak and even the current Islamic State Caliphate in the Middle East is standing and is being held up by the people of the rural and country sections of the region. Osama Bin Laden and his organization built their power while depending on rural people while their opposition was the people of the urban areas and the city ruling governments. Even Al-Baghdadi II, creator and first leader of ISC, found most of his support from the poor and rural people. He applied the same diplomatic mechanisms in Iraq and Syria that Prophet Muhammad had applied during the tribal wars to unite the Arabs of the Arabian Peninsula.

This perspective plays an important part in the advancements between the urban and rural areas, which leave rural societies behind while others advance and live very classy lifestyles. Until all people have the same privileges without critical separations and limitations, we will continue to experience global tensions as the Islamists will keep taking advantage of the financial divisions. Conflicts will continue until poverty is eliminated and the world returns into a peaceful community.

Division and sides

We can also claim that capitalism adds to the division. When looking at the Arab world and comparing capitalism with socialism, we can say that the people of Dubai and UAE enjoy capitalism. Most of the UAE civilians flourished and stayed loyal to their government throughout the decades. At the same time, the Libyan people who lived under the socialist regime for six decades rebelled eventually against the authorities on a massive scale and the revolution started and was kicked off after the 2011 Arab Spring protests. Also, the majority of Saudis enjoys capitalism and is still calm and trying to enjoy peaceful lives, even though we notice some rebelling and jihading tendencies come out of the Saudis here and there. But the Saudi youth, in particular, are facing a different future, as poverty and social problems are increasing.

People wonder why wealthy and educated Muslims like Bin Laden waged rage and wars in the world. Division and dissension within the Islamic world is one of the major points that pushed the Middle Eastern Muslims to rebel and come out in the Arab Spring. As Bin Laden went on to teach and preached the Muslims to unite and fight for their Islamic rights, he did manage to gain followers for the jihadi movement. His actions helped to revive the caliphate (ISC) in 2014, which now claims responsibility for the Sunni Muslims and is expanding its influence all over the world, 25 years after Bin Laden initiated Al-Qaeda.

Islam is just like socialism, holds that every individual has equal rights and that the government's role is to regulate the social, economic and political arenas for the civilians. Islam mandates an obligation by every follower to maintain an Islamic order and a monotheist belief. Therefore, the division of classes among the Muslims is a sensitive matter, which increases the growth of the problem of jihading and Islamic rebelling. Keep in mind that most Muslims live in poor nations.

Christian women converting and mad Muslim men

While there are thousands of Caucasian women in the west who convert to Islam, we have extreme Muslims in the Middle East that are striving for the Islamic rebellion and trying so hard to rebuild their own caliphates. We have the Kingdom of Saudi Arabia, who discriminates against women in the name of Islam and enforces its own Sharia law in the name of Allah (God). Young Saudis end up leaning toward jihadism and rebel, where the radical imams urge Muslims to combat usury, corruption, inequality, bias, corruption etc. The rebellious ideology of Islam is winning here and there, as Muhammad is the main icon for the Muslims. Muhammad is like the godfather for the Muslims to follow. Today, Muhammad is an idol, as imams preach and instruct young Muslims to follow his path and rebel against all tyrannical oppression.

Most Muslim leaders are being confronted by their people, as some of their citizens have joined the Islamic State's ranks. Some in the Western world feels like if this is a 1000-year war. Regardless, thousands of Christians from the western world are converting to Islam.

But for many Muslims, the situation is not acceptable at all. Even Muhammad the self-proclaimed messenger of God would've been upset, embarrassed and disgusted by how his creed is and has been abused. Also, millions of Muslims are troubled by the current situation.

Prevention vs. protection

Protection picks up where prevention leaves off. As violent jihad became a norm in some Muslim societies, it's up to everyone else to prevent it from happening to their own nation and community.

It's fair to assume that the Bush administration was negligent of the American homeland safety, which was breached on 9/11. We, the Americans, had failed to elect the right person for the job back in 2000 to keep us safe from the 9/11 attacks. But it's always good to learn from past mistakes, so we ought to careful in the future.

Beliefs are more efficient than speculations. Beliefs are built on proved knowledge and scientific facts, so everyone should check their beliefs and change their attitudes, if necessary. People's private life systems and behaviors should be reviewed before they end up falling in error and committing wrongful acts. Each individual should commit him or herself to meet a sense of achievement on the personal, social, and even international level, if possible. Civilized nations have to prevent problems from occurring in the first place, or prepare to protect themselves from the consequences of their negligence in second place.

Our destruction

In recent years, it has felt like as if people are losing their faith in education, as the spirit of commitment to education in America is falling behind. Lack of education is our first phase to destruction. Humanity should review and revise the worldwide educational systems. Millions of people still do not comprehend the nature of humans. As humans, we need to act rationally instead of committing reckless acts based on emotion. Negligence is destroying our worldly peace and threatens our future and descendants' future. Abraham Lincoln warned that our destruction could only come from within, so let's be aware.

Peace vs. arrogance

The Red Nations have to rethink their acts and the longer it takes to restart new peace agendas, turmoil will grow and will take over physically and mentally. If the Red Nations keep up the arrogance, future struggles could become more sophisticated and harder to diagnose. New standards concerning peace should take place while considering the current troubled nations. Essential education, health care, and good economies are needed in order to balance the world's psychological well-being. We have to start with the young humans right away, instead of waiting and giving them the need to rebel against society if they fall in the cracks of humanity. If we sit here and don't teach the young ones to act appropriately and behave correctly, many of them might go astray, become savages and become violent people. Low living conditions always forces the poor to turn into wild societies.

The Islamic rebellion and jihadism is a result of our negligence. Negligence by the people and their leaders will result in worse consequences. Every adult of the Red Nations should take the needed measures, get involved and participate peacefully. Everyone should learn how assist their societies or reform them by eliminating the problems at the source, as detailed before. By educating, not war; we can win.

But it takes lots of effort to accomplish the mission, so it's fair to say that the UN should form certain institutions and agencies to service the public and fix the world. Otherwise, we could face worsened situations in the near and far future. Bad future could be World War III.

UNITE! And peace, or World War III

Aftermath of the aftermath

Our world is divided into two classes: the rich north and the dirty south. Mankind needs to be aware of the causes of separation and inequality that exist nowadays. From the desert nomads to the rural villagers, all the way to city dwellers, all must possess civil rights. We must accept everyone. Acceptance has to prevail in order for life to go smoothly and operate in perfection and become full of peace, order and harmony. Then we might be able to regain our perfect status as humans, one nation, under God, indivisible, with liberty and justice for all.

That's what separates the American dream from the American nightmare. We need to fix the current horrible situation of divisions and imbalance within humanity. Understanding and balancing the matter is the most effective way to eliminate social tensions and get rid of repression, struggle and suffering, and hopefully exterminate all of the oppression that exists today. Poverty, lack of knowledge and improper teaching results in impurity. All that will mislead the young generations to the wrong path, and that is where we stand at today.

Today, we stand on the edge of World War III while billions of people are living in denial. The war has already hit home, and the 9/11 attacks are the best proof of the war and the Islamic rebellion's results. It's a very urgent matter that we have to participate in and try to fix before it's too late.

At any given moment, any nation who starts to feel that a government is abusing its power and lacking in its service should take the appropriate measures and legal actions as needed to fix the situation.

Interest groups

Today, we see many civilians standing against the troubling social situations. The occupy everything movement, the 99% movement, the Trump's movement and the anonymous hackers group are all excellent examples of new revolutionary movements that are made of average civilians in reaction to the unaccepted acts of governments and authorities. The people will always rise to respond to mischief and inequality. But the Islamists are on a road of a rebellious movement against a worldly system. The jihad movement has already been initiated, and the Islamic rebellion has been pushing throughout the world since its first reformer, Prophet Muhammad. The self-proclaimed messenger of God triggered off this religious revolution back in the 6th century.

<u>**How far can this go?**</u>

It's obvious that the Islamic State Caliphate is not only challenging the Arab regimes, but it also seems like if it's trying to establish a series of permanent caliphates. Let's just cope with that fact while trying to contain any turmoil that could hit home. This could be a 1,000-year war if mishandled or a 40-year struggle if dealt with correctly.

President Obama started a military campaign against the ISC and in return the ISC called war on us so we should be alarmed. Our war with the ISC is described as 'mission creepy', and we the civilians always wonder why America has to be involved in wars, fights, and violent conflicts that don't even involve our jurisdiction or homeland. We must bring our entire troops home, otherwise we're still sticking our nose where it doesn't belong which keeps damaging us. But if we do what's right, we can win and may be saved within just a few decades.

The Middle East turmoil is sensitive, and everyone who's capable of avoiding the area has a better chance of staying safe. Being there could bring trouble to anyone who intervenes in any wrongful way and sometimes, it harms even those who intervene in righteous ways. We even see aid workers and journalists getting caught in the middle of it.

For the millions of young, desperate and misled Muslims, education, jobs and equality is what they need in their lives, just like all other humans out there. We, as Americans, should focus on our education as well. All children worldwide are in need of the same care and equal opportunities as everyone else, or may rebel if they don't get it.

<u>**Education**</u>

Worldwide higher education should be provided by the United Nations, but it has failed to do so since its establishment in the 1940s. We should force every nation to improve their education and childcare policies. Today, even the Russian public is in need of such improvements. The Russian people are living in very problematic conditions, which increase their envy toward America. The UN has the obligation and primary duty in this matter for the sake of humanity. All central governments have a role as well. Each adult should stand up and take personal action according to his or her particular duty. The Islamic rebellion and terrorism problem can be solved permanently. It may be a

40-year struggle if cured with a coherent strategy or a 1000-year war if dealt incorrectly. But surely, the extreme Muslims are coming at us with their rebellious and Islamic philosophy straight out of the Middle East.

Our children

Meanwhile, we should keep in mind that children are the most important part of this universe. We need to rid the world of extremism and radical influences, especially potential Islamic rebels and jihadists. That's the purpose of the Islamic State: to regulate the jihadists and unite all the young warriors and rebels who come from Sunni Islamic origins. They want to care for their own and their followers who are interested in accomplishing the same cause, which is Islamic liberation and victory. It may be the final wave of jihad, but we assume that these are the early stages of the last Islamic revolutionary jihad, which has strengthened in the past 50 years. It a revolutionary war on existing governments and the jihadists' influence is growing rapidly. That's why caring for children is critical. If the international community doesn't care for them, other radicals will brainwash them and recruit them as foot soldiers.

Every child has some misguided tendencies, and it's up to the society to control them while young, gullible and at risk of adopting radical tendencies. It's the world's duty to correct those traits and teach them the right way to live while their personalities are developing. Then, when they reach the age of maturity, knowledge can help them learn how to live clean, upright, and honorable lives. In that way, as a society, we can eliminate violence from the beginning. We should be teaching the children to reach the main source of peace, right where it originates, which is their consciousness. Otherwise, they might grow up lost and misguided and they will grow up following a path of violence and aggression. Any mistakes will flip back on our society and future, so let's be aware of the consequences of negligence and arrogance.

We must strive for the best so the future generations can grow up better than the current extremists who already have been wrongly taught, and hopefully we can get different results in the future than what we have now. We have reached the pressure point of no return.

Concerning the Muslim civilians

Pakistan is facing the same problem with the Islamic rebellion, and the rebellion has a lot to do with the Pakistani people. The Saudi

Arabian people play another significant role in the rebellion. These two nations are in urgent need of intellectual help. The Iraqi nation has already been consumed. The Syrian people lost stability already. The Jordanian monarch, King Abdullah II, barely gets enough sleep while working hard to manage a nation that is made up of 65-70% war refugees from other local conflicts. Algeria also is at a great risk.

Certainly, civil wars are so common in the Middle East that it's very obvious that World War III will most likely come from there.

We're at the make it or break it time of the 21st century. News will be broadcasted, and stories will become history by 01/01/2101 which is the start of the 22nd century, but life goes on. Even Israel struggles with this infection of madness that has been spreading throughout its territories lately.

Islamic leadership

Christians but Catholics particularly, have the pope to represent them, as Christians mostly follow their churches of faith. While the majority of Muslims are Sunnis and do not follow the Caliph Abu Bakr Al-Baghdadi, they simply obey their secular nations and stay faithful to their local leaders. But that is wrong, according to the striving Islamists, who see the caliphate as the only legitimate statehood to follow. Since the former Ottoman caliphate which was abolished in 1924, few Muslims have participated to form a new one, as Islam instructs. Bin Laden suggested to create a caliphate, and the jihadists reestablished it in 2014.

As the Islamic rebellion was progressing, the Islamic jihadists in Iraq and Syria managed to establish a new caliphate, and so they formed one and elected a new caliph. Concerning uniting Babylon to Mesopotamia, what the Baathist weren't able to do back in the 1930s and 40s; with the help of the jihadists and Islamic rebels, Al-Baghdadi II did it in 2013 and 2014, within a 3-4 year timeframe. According Islam, it's a positive move and should be supported by all Muslims. Muhammad himself combined religion and state (mosque and policy) in his caliphate. In other words, the mosque is also obligated to recommend the Muslims to build a caliphate or support it if possible. From 1924 until 2014, no caliphate has existed. It is not an obligation to be a caliph; it is a favored role by the radical Muslims. It's a volunteered position, and that's why the jihadists are striving to be a caliph nowadays.

UNITE! And peace, or World War III

Since the Muslims haven't had an appointed successor of Islam since the 1920s, a new one had to come in, eventually. A leader was needed in the Middle East for the jihadists and their governance, and that's what we saw in 2014. In that sense, the new Caliph Al-Baghdadi II was elected by the Islamic jihadi council to be a Muslim nation prince and a successor to Prophet Muhammad's duty. That's why he did his task by inviting the rest of the Muslims from around the world to join, welcoming them with the new Islamic citizenship. Today, Muslims have the option to disregard their nationalities, if they wish, and migrate to the caliphate. Al-Baghdadi II was born in 1971 in western Iraq. He's an Arab who was a mosque cleric and imam until the 2003 Iraq war, where he was imprisoned on the suspicion of insurgency activities.

Al-Baghdadi II is an Islamic scholar who earned a Ph.D. degree in Islamic studies in 2000. He is from a Sunni family, who supposedly, traces its bloodline back to Prophet Muhammad. As shown on the back cover of the book, Al-Baghdadi II is the fifth presumed predecessor of the hidden Mahdi. Bin Laden was the first, Al-Zarqawi was the second, Al-Baghdadi I was the third, Al-Masri was the fourth and so the fifth imam is Al-Baghdadi II. Since the formation of Al-Qaeda in 1988 by the global jihadi council, the movement was able to upgrade its operation and take over lots of territories. That's why the jihadists reestablished the current caliphate in 2014 in Iraq and Syria, which also is still expanding. On the back cover of the book, the mysterious 12 imams are listed with the presumed 1st five imams, from Bin Laden to Al-Baghdadi II.

Other than the caliph of Sunni, the Shiite Muslims, who make up around 7% of Muslims, have their own leader. He's also known as the Ayatu-Allah. The problem is that the international community considers these Islamic leaders to be radicals, so Muslims stand with no choice but to sit around and watch the drama that goes on. It's very possible that Armageddon will be a final war between Iran and Israel, as Iran is building a massive war arsenal to wage the war of their 12th imam, better known as the imam Mahdi. Some believe that the Mahdi, who Mahmoud Ahmadinejad has bragged about before, is one of the Anti-Christs' that is described in the prophecies. In the 1970s, Ayatu-Allah Kumaini has claimed that he has "brought the Islamic rebellion".

In other words, there's no unity between the 1.7 billion Muslims except the Quran. The philosophy of Muhammad instructs to revive the jihad against oppression and rebel to form Islamic caliphates. The caliph is supposed to use the Sharia of Muhammad for his legislation. He must be able to fully understand the objectives of the Islamic law and be dedicated to the protection of the five Principles of Islam, which are life, religion, intellect, family lineage and property. That's how deep Islam goes and is just a simple proof of the great program and system which was put to work by the great philosopher of Arabia, Prophet Muhammad. The matter is so complex and so tangled up and confuses Muslims to the point that some Muslims went crazy after seeing it shatter in the early 1900s as the Ottoman Empire caliphate collapsed.

For the Muslims, other than the Holy Lands which the Quran speaks of, they have no relation to Islam, for the simple fact that most of them live under either secular governments or tyrant dictatorships. Muslims are Muslims because they choose to practice it. Many Islamic regimes, like Saudi Arabia, impose harsh restrictions on *ijtihad*, which means personal Islamic striving. *Ijtihad* means that a Muslim must stick to the Quran, follow the Islamic mass movement and participate with the rest of the Muslims by obeying the caliph and his jihad.

Tyrannical Islamic regimes implement restrictions by posting limits on individual freedoms. These governments, take Iran for another example, are against the modification and personal interpretation of Islam to accommodate modernity. They believe this accommodation signifies a surrendering to westernization, as secularization is deemed evil. Therefore, secular regimes promote modernization and advancement while some nations of Islam promote hatred against the laws of the western world. That's the reason Al-Baghdadi II was made a caliph by the jihadists, so the Muslims can listen to his words and obey him to attain an Islamic liberation. Islam instructs Muslims to obey the caliph, starting off with the dedicated and jihading Muslims, and then the moderate Muslims, all the way to the careless and sloppy Muslims. If not, they will be subjected to the Islamic court of law (if available) and face allegations, as disciplinary and punitive actions could be enforced.

Additionally, it is important to note that Islamists such as Osama Bin Laden supported mass jihad which would include millions of jihadists at once. Bin Laden criticized the Saudi regime for disallowing free Islam and imposing harsh restrictions on the successful free practice of Islam and *ijtihad*. Thus, Bin Laden believed in striving for the implementation of Islamic jihad for the millions of the Saudi people. He believed that it was his personal duty as a loyal Muslim to rebel and initiate a jihadi campaign, which he anticipated that he must accomplish. Bin Laden claimed that the Gulf War and the American intervention in it was the breaking point in the Islamic rebellion, and thus he reacted.

An Islamic crusade, per se

"I have a solution" Bin Laden said. Wars are a strange tactic but the Islamic rebellion is taking a solid stand in that mission, as seen. That's how the Muslims steadily are trying to find a leader to fend off their liberties and bring them success and victory in the Holy Lands. For Jerusalem; we'll just call it the disputed land of the Abrahamite cousins.

A convenient approach to understand Bin Laden's point of view is to look at Pope Urban II and his attempt to liberate the Holy Lands, which became known as the First Crusade. The same way Pope Urban II faced political problems and struggles with Henry IV, King of the Germans, is very similar to the political problems that Bin Laden faced with the Saudi monarch. Both Pope Urban II and Bin Laden were out to prove a point by initiating religious campaigns and holy wars.

Young Muslims

Saudi Arabia has its own Islamic sharia regarding executing people and beheading them in public, which drives the inhabitants crazy and has its toll on the Saudi people and youth. Even Bin Laden grew up interested in radical Islam voluntarily for the simple fact that his family raised him as a conservative Muslim. He also felt that he had a holy duty to accomplish with the millions of dollars he inherited, that he ended up investing in promoting jihad and forming Al-Qaeda.

Most of Saudi youth already hates their tyrannical government and is willing to overthrow it in a heartbeat, if possible. Most of the Saudi youth want to strive also, and it's the dream of many young Saudis nowadays. Young Muslims want to liberate the Islamic world from all tyrannical regimes and turn them into a united Islamic caliphate.

The Islamic philosophy itself, which Muhammad introduced, calls people to rebel against oppression and be harsh on crooks, cruel monarchs and corrupted regimes. The Muhammadan philosophy, along with the history of the former Islamic caliphates and how they formed says it all. The spirit of the Islamic rebellion is the core factor of radicalization, extremism and terrorism as well.

The Muslim leaders who allowed their nations to reach this level of instability are the main cause of the problem. They're the ones who abuse their powers, neglect their people and misuse Islam.

Under the current Saudi regime, hundreds of young Saudis are rebelling and becoming jihadists every day. Iraq, Jordan, Syria, Egypt, Algeria, Sudan and the Arabian Gulf countries are the leading producers of radical Islam. It grows on their lands, under their governments' noses, and between their average citizens. Is that America's fault? No! Even America was struck by Islamic jihadists who came from the Middle East. Radical Islam was there before the 9/11 attacks but was ignored and neglected by the Muslim leaders and western nations all along.

But surely, concerning the young Muslims from the western world, their confusion; with the combination of their isolation and hearing about the Islamic battles in the Middle East, might be for some, very attractive and exciting which will make them more attracted to the Islamic rebellion. Some might also rebel, especially if he or she has social, financial or emotional problems. Then young Muslims, who struggle socially, might commit jihad and die in the process of war. Today, thousands of young western Muslims join the Islamic State Caliphate and fight for the sake of the Islamic liberation.

Isn't that the scariest case today? When lost souls and young people enter wars? Shouldn't that be a warning sign for us?

Why does the Saudi monarchy raise mad men?!?

It's time for the Saudi regime to be replaced with a more efficient government for the Arabs. The Saudi people could become the victims of the Islamic rebellion, as many Saudi families have lost their children for getting involved in the rebellion. A regime change from a monarchy to a republic, as the Saudi people wish, will be the most efficient for them instead of the current grower of radical Islam. Today, Saudi Arabia is the #1 jihadist, terrorist and Islamic rebel producer country in the world.

Why should the world wait for more Saudi Islamic rebels to wage Islamic wars and raise conflicts if we live in the 21st century where humanity is enjoying the best advancement ever? It's time for a change, from a failed kingdom to a successful theodemocratic republic.

Why, after all the world wars and mass conflicts, is the Saudi government still allowing Islam to be misused and abused and grow radicals that inflict harm on humanity? Isn't it time for the world community to restore logic and convenience to the Saudi Arabian people as some of them still live in the dark ages?

The Saudi Arabian form of government, a monarchy, is the main reason for Islamic radiciziation among the Saudi youth. It's about time to free the Saudi Arabian people, and if the Unites States does not assist the Saudi people, the ISIS caliphate will move in.

Let's be clear, the Saudi Arabian tyrannical dictatorship is the central problem that has fueled the Islamic rebellion since the 1950s. If Iran is the central problem of the Shiite sect, then Saudi Arabia's governing regime is the central producer of the current jihadism of the Sunni world. That's why the Saudi youth are rebelling as we witness. Sixteen Saudis (including Bin Laden) were involved in the 9/11 attacks.

Since the Saudi government has let its people down and dragged the world into its swamp, it is necessary to change the Saudi regime and tyrannical system as soon as possible. That's the best possible way to eliminate radical Islam from that region of the world. Then hopefully humanity will be able to contain the next wave of Islamic terror attacks. Better yet, we have to save the Muslim youth from joining the next military operations conducted by the Islamic rebels and jihadists.

The Saudi people have had enough of it. That's why thousands of young Saudis are on the edge and are eager to rebel, as they're taught to support Islam and engage in jihad and strive for the Islamic liberation.

How can we prevent the next wave of Islamic terror attacks for the next 100 years from hitting home? Shouldn't we start working on preventing such attacks as soon as possible? Why wait until it's too late?

Muslim imams' hottest topic

There are thousands of imams at mosques, who steadily preach about apocalyptic Islam, especially on Friday mass prayers. The reminder of Armageddon and the holy wars cover a big part of their weekly indoctrinations. While some call it preaching, it brainwashes the lost souls. Shiites do more of it; in general, as they claim that the scenario of Armageddon is already prevailing and they're waiting for the Mahdi.

UNITE! And peace, or World War III

There are three types of imams and mosques concerning this situation. First and most dangerous are the dying imams, those impoverished ones who call for direct and physical jihad since they're the ones who are starving and struggling financially in the first place. Then we have the rich Muslims and mosques that finance the jihad and contribute with their cash and sympathy. Finally, we have the middle-class imams and Muslims, who fall in between and, for the most part, ignore the jihad calls and worry more about their kids and future. But the question about the black banners, that apocalyptic Islam speaks of, has been fulfilled which became apparent to the world in 2014.

The black banners legend is an Islamic prediction that Armageddon will occur in a time when an Islamic army that bears the black banners of Muhammad will march from east Arabia and will fight until Jerusalem is won. The current caliphate (ISC) is located east of Jerusalem as it is based in Syria. These facts give Islamic State Caliphate the assumption that they're the warriors that the prophetic apocalypses spoke of. The Islamic State Caliphate has claimed that it consists of the men who will wage the Holy War of Armageddon until they raise the black banners on temple mount in Jerusalem. The Islamic State Caliphate also believes that they're conducting the end of times biblical scenario. It's one of the imams' hottest topics nowadays.

The Janissaries rebellion

The Janissaries were an elite infantry unit that formed the Ottoman Sultan's troops and bodyguards, which were created in 1383. They began as slaves taken from the European Christians (Romans) and were subjected to strict discipline and wore an army uniform. They were paid salaries and pensions upon retirement and formed their own civil askari (soldier) class. They became first-class citizens of a special military assembly since they were superior and able bodied. Most were non-Muslims because it was not permissible for the Muslim Sultans to enslave a Muslim. But they eventually became one of the ruling classes of the Ottoman Empire due to their skills and talents, rivaling the Ottoman aristocracy and rebelling against it just a few hundred years later.

The Ottomans enslaved non-Muslim boys, notably Anatolian and Balkan Christians, by collecting them in an annual procedure. Once in a while, the Ottomans would send the military to abduct the boys, sons of the Christians in the villages of the Balkans. Some were converted to Islam with the primary objective of employing the ablest children for the military or civil services of the Sultan, especially into the Janissaries' formations.

Sultan Salim II allowed the Janissaries to marry in the 1560s, undermining the exclusivity of loyalty to the Ottomans. By 1622, the Janissaries were a serious threat to the Ottoman Empire. As the Janissaries became aware of their value, they began to request a better life. By the early 17ᵗʰ century, the Janissaries had such reputation and power that they dominated the Ottomans' government positions. They became able to mutiny and dictated governing policies, which hindered efforts to modernize the army structure. They also became able to change Sultans as they wished through palace coups. They even made themselves landholders and tradesmen. Eventually, the Janissaries began extorting money from the Ottomans as business and family life replaced their martial fervor, and ultimately their effectiveness as combat troops decreased. Through their greed and indiscipline, they became a law unto themselves and became weak against modern European armies, as they became very ineffective on the battlefield as a fighting force. With time, the northern borders of the Ottoman Empire slowly began to shrink southwards after the second Battle of Vienna in 1683.

In 1807, a Janissary revolt deposed Sultan Salim III, who had tried to modernize the army along the Western European lines. The modern army Salim III created was the newly reformed order, Tanzeem. The Janissaries killed Salim III based on their accusations that the Sultan failed to obey the religion of Islam. The Janissaries' abuse of power, military ineffectiveness, resistance to reform along with their costy salaries, had become intolerable for the Ottomans by the late 1700s.

In 1826, most of the 135,000 Janissaries revolted against Mahmud II, but the rebellion was suppressed. The Janissary rebellion leaders were executed and their possessions confiscated by the Sultan. As leaders were killed, many members were deported to Europe or imprisoned, and so the Janissary corps was disbanded and replaced by a Muslim military force. Thus the elite order came to its end. The same scenario is being repeated today by the jihadists who come out of the western world. The next quatrain explains how.

UNITE! And peace, or World War III

Today, Muslims are rebelling for a caliphate

Current Islamic rebels are rebelling and jihading against their nations as they're advancing and gaining power. Bin Laden, Al-Awlaqi, Al-Zarqawi and the thousands of Islamic rebels under those men are best compared with the old situation with the Janissaries, who learned the rules of the game from their opposition and flipped back against them. The current number of Islamic rebels in the western world is very low, but the future may differ, as more Muslims might become radicalized while other Muslims are being subjugated in the Middle East by cruel regimes and governments.

The same way the Janissaries used their experience and knowledge to rebel against the Ottomans is the same way we see thousands of Muslims use their experience and learning from the Western world to flip and target those same Western nations. From social media like YouTube and Twitter, to advanced health care and modern war techniques and weaponry, jihadists and Islamic rebels have taken the advanced American and European technologies and turned the tables on the Western world. Today, we have the Islamic State Caliphate and other jihadists who are attacking the western world with the same tools and skills that they learned and obtained from the west.

Islam has a conservative philosophy that rejects coveting, usury, high interest rates and such issues, but that does not prohibit the caliphate from owning a lot of capital and loot. The Muslims who are striving to build a caliphate are seeking to form a massive empire with a powerful central government. This sounds like socialism, but its Islamic socialism. On the contrary, the Islamic rebellion's goal is to build a united, wealthy, and strong Islamic central government, meant to handle the public's issues and afford public spending for the caliphate. In the caliphate, all are treated equally, so it's the system of Islamic socialism. Combining Islamic socialism with western advancement enabled the current caliphate to rise and shine. That's how the Islamic rebels and Al-Qaeda reached five out of their six goals off the jihad list, which is to build and reestablish the caliphate.

By learning from the Western world, the Islamists now have educated people who were taught economics and democracy by the western world, who the Islamic State Caliphate is recruiting.

UNITE! And peace, or World War III

Flip-back, the Islamic renaissance/rebellion

The same way the Ottomans showed the Janissaries how to succeed, which strengthened the European renaissance, is the same scenario that's occurring now. Today, many western Muslims are passing knowledge about social reform and technological advancement, who are not copying the west, but are learning the basic codes of ruling a modern society. Nowadays, Muslims from the Western world simply move to the Middle East and rebel against their opposition. What's happening now is what we may call the Islamic Renaissance, but in this case we align such western Islamic rebels and jihadists with the Islamic rebellion, since they have structural plans and agendas that were placed by Osama Bin Laden. That's how we can relate by looking at all the western Muslims, who are rebelling randomly out of a rejection of the current governmental regimes and waging these religious wars and rebellions.

America, tame your sheep!

A comparable event to the Islamic rebellion that occurred in the past is the revolutionary movements of the European medieval nations, best known as the Renaissance. The Janissaries were a big part of the Renaissance. The Janissaries, who were enslaved Europeans, eventually rebelled and strengthened the European Renaissance and flipped the tides on the Ottomans. The Janissaries learned and gained information about the Ottomans and revolted eventually and helped the Renaissance, and contributed by helping the Christians of Europe to regain power.

America is the shepherd of the world. America needs to tame its allies, such as Saudi Arabia, Yemen, Egypt, Iraq, and such Muslim countries; because some of their citizens are flipping on the Western world the same way the Janissaries rebelled against the Ottomans.

Islamic socialism

As mentioned before, the Islamic socialist order was the one adopted by the successors of Muhammad, who also claimed to hold the monotheist creed and ideology of Abraham the Patriarch.

Those Abrahamic ideas that turned into the religious doctrine of Muhammad are what brought forth the Islamic caliphate and its succession. We can refer to it as the Islamic socialist society, where the old caliphate usually came to help troubled cities, wherever people needed such systems of governance. People always try to find better life systems through the use of the ideologies, and the old Muhammadan socialist system provided it entirely.

From the 5th to the 7th centuries, from Arabia all the way to Spain and to China, Islam spread throughout the Old World within 100 years; by the sword and also by spreading Islamic socialism.

Comparing how we handled the KKK vs. managing the ISC

Some say that the Federal Bureau of Investigation, made out of Christian white men, dismantled the KKK and destroyed their abilities to inflict harm on others. That does not mirror the Muslim kings, princes, presidents and rulers who failed and are still failing to combat extremism on their own lands. Muslim leaders allow their citizens to harm others, like the 9/11 attacks, for example.

The FBI is a successful agency with loyal agents, while the Muslim leaders are failing rulers and corrupted politicians. Every ruler and leader who claims to be a Muslim is obligated to diffuse the problem, or it's time for them to step down. But many of the Muslim leaders won't step down because they're straight dictators and tyrants. Today, the United States' government is trying so hard to help the failing Iraqi government, who stood around and didn't help beat down the crisis within its own jurisdiction. Better yet, the Iraqis are using America as a bodyguard to protect the governmental members while they earn salaries and enjoy a wealthy life as they're still failing their people!

Egypt is another example; as Egypt's failing leaders are tearing that country apart. Today, Egypt is under martial rule. The Middle East is collapsing and eventually it will be a victory for the Islamists. The jihadists have been trying to beat those secular regimes for the past seven decades, since they "failed to rescue Jerusalem and the Palestinian people". Toppling the Middle Eastern regimes was the fourth goal on Al-Qaeda's jihad list. And the Islamic rebellion doesn't stop there.

The governmental system of Saudi Arabia, which is the mother of radical Islam, should be switched, as the whole regime should be fixed into a theodemocratic republic for a better future and a peaceful world. Saudi Arabia and the way it allows jihad to be exported from its homelands is a painful example. Millions of Saudis are waiting for the black banners of the Islamic State Caliphate to arrive and break the border between the Arabs in their lands. They see that the ISC as the last chance for freedom that they may obtain against the current Saudi tyranny.

That is the core of the matter and the head of the snake. Our federal government was combating the KKK, who received care educationally, medically and socially in a stable economy and lives. On the contrary, the current Muslim and Arab autocrats steadily neglect their people, as their young generations are living in poverty, which intensifies their emotional affection toward jihadism as they might be surrounded by radical Islamic people. That usually leads them to grow up and adapt the Islamic rebellious ideology, which gives them a new form of hope instead of living under tyrant leaders who are leaving them behind for the western world to deal with. That's why imams are sending rebels and jihadists toward the Islamic rebellion right and left. Today, there are more than 1.5 million imams with 1.7+ billion followers.

That's why we see the Islamic rebellion gaining supporters and becoming much bigger, as young Muslims go to preachers, who bring them one step closer by instructing them to join the Islamic rebellion and support it physically if possible, and if not, support it financially. Some might say that this war is between the imams and all non-Muslims.

The Islamic rebellion is expanding quickly due to the negligence of the Muslim leaders, who also are the central cause of the problem.

Most Islamic jihad fronts today falls under the Islamic State Caliphate, and some jihadist groups have formed states of their own under the Al-Baghdadi II's authority, and the caliphate goes on.

So America did suppress the KKK, but America is losing it to the Islamists and jihadists. Truly, we have mismanaged to win the war.

The itch

By now, America feels the itch of young Muslims pushing for an Islamic reform and refreshment, hoping to bring back the united Islamic identity. If the Islamic State Caliphate succeeds and gains control over the Islamic world, this rebelling tendency could increase very sharply and could grow 100 fold. According to this assumption, if the Islamic State Caliphate is made up of eight to ten million residents today, the size could go as high as one billion members within the next 70-200 years. By now, thousands of poor, broken, mad, sick and even devout

Muslims are pledging allegiance to Al-Baghdadi II to obtain the new Islamic identity and citizenship under the caliphate's discretion.

The Islamic States Caliphate (ISC) project

The Islamic States Caliphate enterprise has franchise states in Syria, Iraq, Libya, Egypt, Algeria, Saudi Arabia, Yemen, and other areas in the Middle East. Today, there are Islamic States in West Africa, Central Asia, and Southeast Asia. The Islamic State Caliphate is currently made up of more than 25 separate states. They accomplished the unity of the caliphate, under the banner of the Islamic State, which set Al-Raqqah as the capital, and placed the successor Al-Baghdadi II as the leader and caliph of the Islamic nation.

Rejection of the Islamic State Project

Upon the reestablishment of the current caliphate, many international governments and rulers opposed the regime, which caused the power struggle between the Islamic State and such opposing governments. The UN does not approve the statehood of the caliphate. The Islamic State Caliphate is considered as illegitimate under international law and also is listed as a terrorist organization and has been battled by the Red Nations since August 8, 2014.

How real is the Islamic State?

The Islamic State has an Islamic court system that rules by Muhammad's Sharia law, and that's the essential part of the true Islamic caliphate. Courts are where justice begins, so the Islamic State Caliphate brings Islamic justice; both personal and social. Most Muslim countries have secular court systems and secular laws, which contradict Islam, as Islamists label those systems as hypocritical, all the way to the leaders who regulate such judicial systems. From Osama Bin Laden to Al-Baghdadi II, the jihading movement has been through many stages until the grand reopening announcement of the caliphate on July 4th, 2014. That was authenticated because it was broadcasted on the internet, and many television and radio stations throughout the world.

The Islamic State Caliphate has established Islamic governance over its lands according to their court system. The Islamic State Caliphate has a consultative council where matters are to be settled by the majority's vote, which leaves the Islamic democracy in full effectiveness and labels it as an authentic caliphate. It is very legitimate according to the Islamic philosophy that is recorded in the Quran, which contains Muhammad's prophetic doctrine.

Apparently many Islamologists and Islamic scholars don't approve the legitimacy of the Islamic State Caliphate, but that's understandable. That's because they're not up to the real Islamic quest, which would get them in trouble with the international community. That causes the Muslim youth to understand the insincerity of those rejecters of their own Islamic teachings. The young and eager Muslims go on to follow the Islamic State Caliphate and practice what Al-Baghdadi II preaches, since he practices what he preaches.

The Islamic scholars' weakness by not backing up their cause literally against the Muslim tyrants and dictators enables the Islamic State Caliphate and other jihadists to affirm their seriousness which shows their commitment and dedication to other Muslims. That's why younger Muslims from all around the world turn against their local weak imams and choose to rebel and follow the caliph of the Islamic State Caliphate. In other words, Muslims recognize the authenticity of the Islamic State Caliphate. But while most of the older imams choose to stay at home and watch the movie from far away, many other younger and eager Muslims go on to get involved in the action. That's how poverty, depression and oppression blow up, as in a suicide attacker that has his or her point to prove to the world, to show how serious he or she is about his or her Islamic rebelling and jihading cause. The jihadists and Islamic rebels are dead serious and they steady announce their plans and goals to the public.

The Islamic State is very Islamic and legitimate according to the true Islam of Muhammad, and that is a significant turning point, especially for future Muslims. The problem comes with its war. Muslim leaders have already called the conflict World War III as they all know that their time is short and is running out. Now, Muslim leaders are trying to collect as much wealth as possible before they get ousted. By now it is already a global conflict since the Red Nations make up about half of the world. The armed conflicts have been contained in general but not limited to the Middle East. That's why it seems as if there's a cold war between the western powers and the radical Islamic imams and their fellow rebels; as the Islamic State Caliphate is their proto symbolic country. Let's make it clear, any imam is an Islamologist, and there are millions of Islamologists in the world while Al-Baghdadi II is the grand imam of the caliphate. He's an Islamologists and is the current caliph.

The other 1.7 billion Muslims

While the current Arab leaders are buying time to gain affluence, the rest of the civilian Muslims have their personal choice, whether they would turn to the Islamic State Caliphate to gain the new Islamic citizenship or just disregard the invitation and continue as nationals of other nations. In Iraq, today, this issue is creating a life and death problem for millions of people. It's even causing a sectarian war somewhat.

In Iraq, people are facing two options: either pledge allegiance and submit to the Islamic State Caliphate or stay a renegade and become a challenger of the caliph and his armies. This matter has also spread throughout the Middle East as well, and that surely terrifies the Arab and Muslim leaders of losing control over their jurisdictions.

Although only about a million Muslims around the world seem to be interested and support the Islamic State Caliphate, the rest of the 1.7 billion Muslims are left hanging between the grips of other governments and the caliphate's mercy.

The caliphate is accepting converts and newcomers who wish to join the Islamic State Caliphate. According to the annual reports of the Islamic State Caliphate, hundreds submit to their Islam willingly.

For instance, we learned of an old French man who converted to Islam a long time ago. Once the caliphate was reestablished in 2014, he moved to Al-Raqqah and applied for citizenship from the Islamic State Caliphate. He then was authorized, and he finally declared that he was an approved citizen of the Islamic State Caliphate and was no longer a citizen of France. More concerning newcomers and converts will be explained in the next quatrains and centuries.

The August 8, 2014, declaration of air war

The Red Nations coalition began an air strike campaign against the Islamic State Caliphate, and in return, the Islamic State Caliphate declared war on the Red Nations and their belongings.

The air force deployment of August 8, 2014, led by President Obama, is at an open-ended war with the Islamic State Caliphate. Today, after decades of the war on terror, America is back at war with more terrorists.

My sources have affirmed that the air campaign against the Islamic State is failing miserably. The costs had been valued at several millions of dollars a day, with around four billion dollars in the first year alone and a few hundred civilians killed during these bombings so far.

Staying true to our self is very necessary regarding our military intervention within the Islamic world. We must always keep in mind that the Islamic jihadists will always use any and every civilian death as a propaganda tool against us. Any civilians' death caused by our American army or air forces will be a victory for the jihadists.

For example, Mrs. Hillary Clinton has said that Mr. Donald Trump's rhetoric against Muslims will be used by the jihadists as a recruiting tool. This case might be true; but a worst scenario would be once children or innocent bystanders get killed on accident by a drone strike that was supposed to target militants or terrorists. In that case, the accident killings of such innocent lives would be a direct recruiting tool by the jihadists who would use those accidental deaths to entice madness and promote jihad and rebelling. The jihadists would claim that such accidental killings are deliberate acts of killings Muslims. Either way, the world community must come together, unite, and end all the blood shed permanently. Otherwise, we will be facing World War III with just a few decades from now.

UNITE! And peace, or World War III

Since the 9/11 attacks, the American public has been somewhat confused about how we should treat the Islamic terrorism problem. To keep it simple, uniting and confronting the Islamic rebelling problem head on is the wisest option that we may have. We could continue the war on terror for decades and centuries if we wish, but that may not eliminate the Islamic rebellion and its causes. Uniting with the peaceful Muslims, introducing a peaceful political solution and setting a plan for the Islamic world would bring healthier results than fighting a rebellious ideology. Otherwise, this could be a 1000-year war, with millions to die in it, which eventually would become known as World War III.

9. The caliphate, humanity, and the rest
Economy, industry and market of the Islamic State Caliphate

Black gold, white gold, and even yellow gold are tradable in the current caliphate. Today, black gold, best known as petroleum, is the number one good produced by the Islamic State Caliphate.

From all around the world, up to 60% of oil reserves are in the hands of people who hold Islam as their religion. That's one of the main reasons that motivate the Islamic rebellion, which is to take over such valuable industry. The Islamic rebels intend to regain full control of the oil, which is opposed by those who are currently in control of the industry: the OAPEC and its members. It's a whole new issue that's also causing conflict between the Islamic rebellious movements and the governments in the Middle East.

It is absurd how the UN committee is not controlling the natural resources of this planet and leaving the average people to fight over it. The UN is letting random governments and private parties use natural resources instead of serving it fairly to the world's community. Until the world finds an agency that regulates natural resources, the feuds will continue as people will fight to take over it.

Islamic empathizers

Today, many avid lovers of Islam tend to set off and get directly involved and go on to join the Islamic rebellion by joining the ranks of the Islamic State Caliphate (ISC) in the Middle East and elsewhere, while many jihadists are striking the Red Nations right at their homelands.

If the Red Nations continue the war with the Islamic rebels and jihadists, especially of the Islamic State, the consequences could be harsh and disastrous. In general, civilians will stay endangered, soldiers at war, and governments at tight times. The economies of the Red Nations on edge, stability at risk and security is low. Harmony in the Red Nations could be disrupted, the order could be lost and peace could be broken.

All throughout the Red Nations, if the conflict reaches home, infrastructure could be damaged, markets could be devastated and civilizations could be troubled. By now, the Islamic rebellion is in a conclusive altercation with the Red Nations. The Islamic State Caliphate is the heart and main breath of the Islamic rebellion, so any more war with the caliphate will squeeze the rebels, which in return might bring more fatal consequences to the opposition. It might even cause more terror attacks on the western world. That's a fair warning for whoever seeks guidance in this book.

The civilian residents of the Islamic State Caliphate

Any Muslim who resides in the Islamic State Caliphate, abides the Sharia law, does his or her job and contributes to the community will be able to use the offered benefits and opportunities by the caliphate.

Many of the newcomers to the caliphate must feel overwhelmed with the new nationality. They're probably looking forward to enjoy the new belonging while trying to prove themselves with the new Islamic identities that they're experiencing.

Any new Muslims that come from any other Islamic foundations or secular countries were reborn into the rebellion. It is not only a source of dignity and pride for them but also a life-changing event that shapes a new way for their future. The best bet is that they will get to work on the caliphate, its survival, conflicts, and expansion. The caliphate is active, so newcomers will be put to use sooner or later; just like the volunteering original civilians who live under the current rule of the caliphate's jurisdiction.

Surely the Islamic State Caliphate is at war with the Red Nations, so the caliphate's residents should be aware of the militaristic combats that take place. The Red Nations are using military tactics to fight the caliphate, and residents should be careful of gunfire and explosions 24/7. The risks of joining the caliphate should be advised to the lost souls.

Other civilians of the caliphate

As the conflict has been identified, the civilians and residents of the caliphate are under the fire of 60+ governments of the Red Nations and other warring factions. The officials of the caliphate are maintaining positions and responding by increasing the intensity of violence as they drown some of their oppositions alive and others get beheaded, burned alive, crucified, lashed, etc. That's why millions of civilians have been fleeing the affected area. Most civilian are fleeing along the Afrasian migration to Europe.

Civilians always fall victims to oppression, but in war, everyone loses. A peaceful approach is urgent. For the caliphate's government officials, jihadists and loyal followers, a world war against them is understood as it gets closer. Even though no one wants to die, it seems that the Islamic State Caliphate acknowledges that it is on a long-term warfare until victory or death.

Just as Hitler was the most contributing factor in World War II, the Islamic State Caliphate seems to be willing to wage another world war; as they believe that it will be beneficial and necessary to gain victory and liberate their Islamic lands. Bin Laden, as mentioned before, invested in the next world war, just as Hitler invested World War II.

Other inhabitants of the Islamic State Caliphate

One of the main causes for opposing the Islamic State by the international community is the risk of public and religious cleansing. Apostasy, idolatry, paganism, heresy, polytheism, atheism, and fidelity are against Islam, therefore, they are prohibited by Islamic law, which the Islamic State Caliphate uses as its legislation for its laws and regulations. As the Islamic State caliphate wants to take over the Islamic world, it creates concerns.

In the caliphate, mosque and state are one. Sworn Muslims are first-class citizens under recognition of the Islamic State Caliphate while non-Muslims are considered second-class citizens.

Sworn Muslims of the caliphate enjoy all rights and privileges provided to the public. Foreigners and non-Muslims are treated as second-class citizens. They are subject to pay a dhimmitude tax and are stripped of any political, religious and militarily powers.

The Islamic State Caliphate is entirely conservative, which is very efficient for the Muslim inhabitants, but the atheists or the opposition will not be tolerated. It's then critical to recognize that not every Arabic person is a Muslim. There are Arab–Jews and others are Christian. The population identity is very critical in this case.

There are more than 550 million Africans who are Muslims, but most of them have not gotten involved in the Islamic rebellion yet. In Nigeria, Boko Haram is an Islamic jihad front, which is under the Islamic State Caliphate's recognition and is called the Islamic State of West Africa. Egypt, Libya, Somalia and Algeria have franchises of the Islamic State Caliphate also. The jihadists liberate the land and simply add them to the caliphate.

The caliphate, humanity, and the rest

The complications of the Islamic rebellion are flowing throughout the world with immense impacts. The rebels can come from many places. For example, up to 50 million Chinese people are Muslims; and it's unknown how many of them are being attracted to the Islamic rebellion.

The Islamic rebellion is relatively global but is very ambitious. Anyone who claims that the Mossad, CIA or Iran created the Islamic State is living in either denial or simply lacks knowledge about the actual origination of the Islamic State Caliphate and the Islamic rebellion that created it. The Islamic State Caliphate has evolved from the Islamic world wars as a result of Bin Laden's effort and jihad.

Financial struggles and poverty are engulfing the Islamic world, which also fuels the Islamic rebellion.

The Muslim rulers that are in charge are the most responsible men, who watch the rebellion hit others but don't care as long as their palaces and mansions stay served by the western soldiers and fooled governments. Those leaders are the ones that are raising the Islamic rebels daily in their countries while they're in office and leaving the terror to grow on their watch. They must be replaced as soon as possible with just republics, and hopefully the people will appoint whom they wish to lead them to do a better job and fix the problems throughout the Islamic world.

The Islamic State Caliphate is authentic and is 100% Quranic

A caliphate upon the prophetic doctrine of Muhammad and his Sharia law is where the Islamic State Caliphate stands at today. The Islamic State Caliphate is 100% Islamic, and Muslims who deny that fact obviously are not speaking about the accurate reality. Egypt, for example, allows Alcohol consumption, which is against Islam. While the Islamic State Caliphate is 100% Islamic according to the Muhammadan Sharia laws, Egypt is the perfect example of a secular government. The Islamic State Caliphate is completely Islamic.

Whatever the Islamic State Caliphate does is based on Islamic reason, so denying the Islam of 'ISIS' is very misleading. Whoever labels the Islamic State Caliphate as un-Islamic is either confused or maybe does not understand the Islamic Rebellion and its results and causes. Any Muslim who denies that fact is just either in shock of how the current caliphate came about, or is just simply not embracing the authentic Quranic Islam. Any Muslims who is denying the Islam of the Islamic State Caliphate is living in total denial. This may sound unfair to the 1.7 Muslims, but it is the truth. If not, they probably lack knowledge about Islam and are uninformed of what they follow. The Indian scholar Maudidi claimed that "not more than 0.001% of Muslims know what Islam actually is". Millions of Muslims are oblivious of what they follow.

War times of the Islamic State Caliphate

When an armed conflict occurs and civil tranquility cracks off, the Islamic State will declare a war emergency and will start the army recruitment in order to meet the military needs to strengthen the ranks of the army. In such situations, the caliphate might encourage Muslims to volunteer and pick up arms in case of any insurgency against the caliphate since it doesn't require army reserves. For Muslims, jihad is optional, not mandatory, as drafting is not allowed in Islam. Non-Muslims are not required to engage in jihad or fight for the caliphate and thus they are free to leave the caliphate's land or fend off for themselves if they wish.

That's what the Islamic State Caliphate is by now. It's more like a jihad front, which also consists of an Islamic statehood as well. The Islamic State Caliphate's doors are wide open to newcomers. So the Islamic State Caliphate has picked up where Al-Qaeda left off.

That's where depressed young Muslims and lost souls, combined with Islamic extremism and the availability of explosives and firepower, make the deadly mix that has been going off recently. Since Bin Laden's support in the 1970s, the jihadists and Islamic rebels have made their statement very clear. They fight for a religious cause which is Jerusalem.

It's almost a full-scale rebellion by now: the stage is set, and the war is on. The Islamic State Caliphate is at war with the Red Nations.

Learning logic vs. brainwashing

Openness and acceptance are keys to gaining control of life. People need to be taught logical behaviors and learn rationality to resist greed, envy and wrath. Love, compassion and empathy should be provided and shown to our descendants. People follow what they learn, but if some children are being brainwashed, this matter could go much further, and the Islamic rebellion could consume the whole world if left

The caliphate, humanity, and the rest

Peacemakers don't lie, break agreements and never betray others. Peacemakers never get mad when they argue with others. These are the traits that will enable us to recognize the peaceful from the hypocrites and liars, so don't be deceived by speech skills and personal accomplishments. Peacemakers answer all questions and never hide.

Today, as we know, there's a disconnection between what leaders say and do, so humanity is in need of a revival of rights, liberties and happiness for all. A peaceful approach is the only possible way to end all wars on this planet and is the best way to go. Every conscious citizen must get involved in selecting the right leadership who will work for the greater good instead of any personal or special interests.

Awfully

Peace is lost in many parts of the world, and apparently, it's a human error that caused such disastrous conditions. Every statesman and politician who hasn't done enough to bring peace is to blame, especially as their communities are also losing. Some parts of the world are being held hostage by awful rulers and their autocracies such as the communists' regimes. The people of China, Cuba, Venezuela, North Korea, Russia, Iran, India etc. have been abused and screwed by wrongful leaderships and communist regimes.

We all know that communism is more like a legalized slavery program under the international community's acceptance. It's all happening right under the UN watch. Billions of people around the world are starving under the UN's sight.

Today's liberals seem too weakened, as democracies are being raped and the poverty in the African nations and the dirty south is the best example. The old British occupation should be blamed, as it promoted colonization, imperialism and controlling others.

The question is whether humanity will ever obtain the necessary freedom. If yes, when and how peaceful will it be to gain total physical and mental freedom, where every human has his or her total personal freedom and private liberties? What the Islamists are doing comes from the core of the jihadism ideology of the Islamic philosophy. It is the theme of Muhammad, who supposedly followed Abraham's creed and used Moses' way to earn freedom and gain peace and independence from evil tyrants. That's according to Muhammad. The truth is that no one gives freedom nowadays; people strive and struggle hard to earn it.

Rest of the world's civilians

There are three types of lifestyles that classify humans today. We have the city dwellers, country farmers, and the natural people.

1. Cities, towns and urban gatherings are where people connect with each other as they're all a part of the civil society.

2. Country farmers and villagers are the people who usually stay in the country and have little contact with the urban areas.

3. Natural people are the people who live out in the nature, such as the desert nomads, indigenous people, and Eskimo. They stay out in the wilderness and have no or very little contact with the civilized world.

While the natural people live in the state of nature, Mother Nature is all they worry about. But the city dwellers are the most important out of the three types of human lifestyles. The importance comes from the activities and the influences that they have on others. The people of the city are the ones who have the most power and are the ones that change the world the most. That's how the urban vs. rural effects take place and differentiate between the people and create the divisions and limitations of comfort and joy.

In general, the more people are confined to a smaller area, the easier they are to be controlled. City residents are the most active and continuously growing populations, which usually results in more problems of social division within a nation. The city people are the intended audience of new innovations and inventions.

City people should be taught and acknowledged that they are a part of a one global chain of cities that are operating the world's economic cycle, which keeps life going.

Within cities, there are criminal tendencies, drugs, oppression, sensitive economies, declining budgets, global corruption, local tensions, personal rejection, governmental dissatisfaction, social rebelling and most are on the rise.

Around the world, communism, socialism, and even the Islamic terrorists, are attacking America from under the carpets. The problem must be fixed before more trouble accumulates as we see today.

Acceptance and openness

Openness and staying informed of facts and realities is totally different from acceptance and approving with such information. You may learn about a subject, but that does not mean that you have agreed to it. Acceptance is paramount.

Acceptance and openness should be understood as necessities of today's life. You can understand a subject, but still, acceptance takes more than just understanding the concept. Respect, as mentioned before, is a sign of acceptance that ultimately brings peace among the people. So being respectful is also necessary.

The best way to have an easier time accepting others is to love the reality that we're all a part of one community of this Earth. Mother Nature is generous and provides for all of us. Loving Mother Earth, accepting the beauty of our existence and obeying all the natural laws are the best ways to enjoy life.

Fear, anger and depression are emotions and mental conditions. Those wishing to do better regarding these emotions have to liberate their attitudes, feelings and thoughts from all the malice, hate, jealousy, madness, wrath, strife and harshness that exists in our world today and instead keep control of the self. Always relax yourself and take it easy. Make sure to conquer yourself first and then look forward to conquering others.

Potential fatal consequences of human error

Many misguided young Muslims have fallen in error while embracing wrongful lifestyles and went on to engage in jihad and Islamic terrorism. Young terrorists also hurt their parents as much as the victims that they attack. It is a menacing fact and needs to be addressed.

The entire world's population must be taken care of, by us as a human community, regardless of any costs. Many tyrannies are actively in effect somewhere in the world as we move on.

For example, China restrains its people into a social order and leaves a tight area for personal liberties. Only a small percentage of people in China have the opportunity to break out of the repression that they're born into. We, the Americans, have much more pleasure in our lives compared to our fellow Chinese people. Such repression and communist restraint are what creates rebellions and revolutions.

Africans who live in poverty are at a significant risk, as the drought situation in Ethiopia (and central Africa) is troubling and brings many problems along. Take Ebola, for example, the longer it was ignored in Africa, the more it risked spreading around the world. The current African migration into Europe is also another problem that the United Nations ignores daily.

Latin America, including Mexico, is in some horrible conditions in many areas, which causes illegal immigration to explode into the United States of America, as we have been witnessing since the 1950s.

For the most part, the Russians have gotten the worst of it out of all the Caucasian nations of this world. The Russian people are having a hard time with their economy and security more than any other white nation there is out there.

Americans, in general, enjoy a free market. A little tax must be paid to Uncle Sam, but the American people enjoy the right to property and wealth to the maximum. Every American has the right to any amount of money and property to keep as he or she wishes to earn by his or her economic participation and hard work.

The American markets are open but they need volunteers to work, invest their money and pay taxes as our democracy entitles them to. Some of these privileges are lacking in Russia, which increases the animosity and envy on us in America by the Soviet-empathizing Russians. These are human errors and must be addressed.

Weak politics and new opportunities

We have an elite class and professional politicians – from the congress all the way to the president – that run the master city, Washington, DC. Still, every American man or woman has the full legal recognition and right to take the lead and run for any official or political position during the election times.

Refreshment in the American political arena is much needed. Dear readers: start training your sons and daughters and get them ready already for such political positions. It sounds like a conspiracy, but it is a righteous plot for all Americans. Plot to fix our country; that's what we should be conspiring on.

Being an American patriot and occupying a political office are two different perspectives. In the case of some politicians, they are there for the money, fame and career. Train your kids, and within a decade or two, all the wrongful and misleading politicians will be long way gone and new people will be needed to replace them. We need to see good action taken; Americans that will make the world proud!

Wake up

Undoubtedly, the arrogant type of American politicians who don't have to worry about monthly bills or kids' college funds like the rest of us, are considered elite compared to us, the average civilians. That upper class that includes the 1% of rich people is getting worn out, and soon the average people will be able to pick up the role. Those rich are simply enjoying America. They are not too worried that many fellow human beings are poor, wretched and living paycheck to paycheck. It's more like if the rich class has enslaved us; the rest of the average Joes. The rich keep cash and large accounts. They feel like they have been rewarded for their good work and responsible behaviors, and once they're in that position, they usually flip and abuse what they have.

That's still not the problem. Better yet, that's how the America's capitalism works, as mentioned before. As it was detailed, 1% of us Americans are rich and wealthy who are enjoying this heaven, just as the little more than 1% of us that are criminals and convicted felons, who are poor and suffering in the jail cell's hell.

While the rest of the population is left hanging between those two groups, some people feel that our government is made up out of a bunch of conspirators. But still, America is more like a corporation who owns the land and runs the business, something for us to realize.

War decisions or peace talks

We still see images of war on TV, and millions have been affected, physically and mentally, by the wars. The American soldiers should be protecting our borders, airports and seaports, not serving in Germany, Japan or Jordan far away from their families and homeland.

But that's the proof of our empire at work. Only empires work that way. Also, no rational person appreciates collective conflicts; which is war. Collective conflicts can be portrayed today as a fight between groups of drunken men in a bar that are swinging back and forth at each other and people are just getting hit; including the innocent bystanders.

Humans need love, honor and respect. What we have today is a lot of gunfire that is being triggered most of the time with the intention of shedding blood. Killing is always a merciless act, regardless of the

115

situation.

As Americans, we need to end all war. Freedom was never enlisted to kill humans, although that's the duty of all armed forces around the world. Soldiers are meant to obey orders and engage in combats, even though they have the right to control themselves and make decisions as they wish.

Methods to use

Applying a better and a broader peace strategy is necessary. Dialect and listening to the needy is a good way to start. Through honest and full conversations, many issues will be brought to the spot light.

Providing proper awareness and keeping transparent are paramount in bringing justice. We must recognize the values, and reach the logical and full solutions to problems in order to have better results. We must introduce adjustments and work with the global community to help bring peace.

The world's community needs to elevate primary life requirements and needs. Maintaining perfection and keeping critical analysis will be helpful to identify the strength of the efforts.

Always ask the experts and listen to all views. Observe the actions and establish full justice. Only conscious people bring the truth of their instinct to help lead and guide their nations.

For a better future

You should stay at peace with others. Greet them properly. Appreciate the air that we consume. Enjoy Mother Nature and do not abuse her. Love Father Nature and respect his highness.

Be honorable, respectful and loyal. Feed the hungry. Be gentle and comfort the struggling humans. Guide the lost, confused and spiritually dead. Respect the elderly and please them. Forgive the sinner and educate the wrongdoers until everyone is purified. Eliminate the wicked and the corrupters. Exterminate the cowardly and traitors. Glorify the virtue and righteous. Protect the weak and support the law. Expose the crooked and venerate the upright. Stand united under the one good man against the scattered oppressive men. Split away far from the ones that encourage irrationality and join the conscious leader. Enforce equality. Reject envy. Love other beings regardless of shape, color, size, type, kind and their relationship to you. Be vigilant, persistent, careful, brave and conscientious.

The people should criticize, inform and convict all the corrupters and wrongful rulers and their governments. Wish for peace and try to gain the peace of mind as much as possible. That is the start to a better destiny.

To our fellow Americans, love your enemies and help the weak. Vote in perfect presidents and politicians, and make sure they are righteous men who do not discriminate or run evil. Look at the empires before America and observe how they were brought down by nations they abused and underestimated.

Yes! Muckraking

Muckraking is criticizing the corruption and scandalous actions of political leaders, which is a way to start fixing the governments, so muckrake and expose the wrongdoers. Perfect existence is built on honesty and everything else will cause crookedness. Perfection will bring peace, and peace will allow perfection. Peace advocates don't lie, don't break agreements, and don't betray promises. Peacemakers never transgress when they're involved in any arguments. Outside these traits, people could be hypocrites with double intentions. Any disconnection between any person's actions and sayings are the signs of hypocrisy and corruption.

The rest of the world: cities, villagers and starters

Some master cities affect the world at massive scales. For example, the financial district of Illinois is located in the city of Chicago. Also Shanghai, Karachi, Delhi, Istanbul, Lagos, Moscow, Cairo, Jakarta, Tokyo, London, Mexico City, New York City, Jeddah and Berlin are great examples of a connected network of urban civilization that exists on the surface of planet Earth. Humans in cities are residing in packed and concentrated patches of land. Governments serve the lands using laws that constitute the rules and regulations made by the inhabitants. Basically, cities are controlled environments for human beings.

Governments rule the city as markets function to serve, produce and service the dwellers. The people who enjoy the most power are the ones in the cities, where urban government officials usually have powerful influence and affect all types of people throughout civilizations.

The Russian government's power in the East Serbian Sea, for

example, and the way the USA controls Alaska are great examples of how people of the city have such great control and power. City leaders rule others and control them even though they might be very far from their locations. In the past, the English people from the master city of London ruled America, Africa, the Middle East and South Asia, as mentioned before.

The British rule and administration of the African territories in the 1800s was directed from the master city of London. London was a master city at some point, but today it's just a very populous civil society, which is known as Greater London. Ancient Rome was another master city, where its people expanded their rule to Jerusalem, Athens, Constantinople and Carthage.

Master cities contribute to technology and technical advancements while the rural people provide the labor, agriculture and produce in return. All that occurs while the city people also affect the natural people, as the Europeans affected the Native Americans in the 1500s after discovering their land. City people also affect desert nomads by using their environment to extract goods, such as oil drilling in the Arabian Peninsula. What the Eskimo go through and the way America bought Alaska and controlled the native people is another good example of a master cities influence. Take the might of Washington D.C., for example. The power of that master city is the greatest around the world today. Washington D.C. is the strongest and most recognized master city from the beginning of human civilization until this day and so it goes.

Logging, mining, oil drilling, land use and such industries affect natural people. But those poor people have no physical power to resist the master cities who invade their environments, so they fall slaves to the masters: the city people.

It would be fair to say that the people of the city usually invade others to sustain themselves and gain their needs and wants. China claims to be a people's republic, while it invades the fundamental human rights and restrains the Chinese people. Such constraining by the communist system of China is still active. Unfair government systems divide the people and create separations, which always come from the city people and their selfish reality.

Moscow is a great example of such a master city, where its

mandates shaped the future with time. Moscow succeeded and was able to export its influence to other nations, which later was known as the Soviet Union.

Whether it was Karl Marx's philosophy or Vladimir Lenin's political work, the ideology of the socialist system directly influenced millions of people. Better yet, billions, such as the Chinese people, the Indians, Brazilians, Vietnamese, Cubans, North Koreans, Venezuelans, etc., are all suffering from communism and socialism. Such influences were developed and spread by the people of the city of Moscow.

So what's the next master city? Mecca? That's what the Islamists wish.

Rural inhabitants and villages

Other than the city people, there are the people of the rural areas and villages.

At any given moment, the world economic cycle could break, the financial markets could collapse, and the daily life routine will pause. That's when plantations will be the best resort to rely on for survival.

The further from the city it is, the more peaceful life will be. Electric power, solar power, wind power and rivers will enable the people to sustain a comfortable life while the cities could turn into slums within a short frame of time. The conditions in New York City during the 1930s great depression are a great example of such dilemmas. Every authority in charge could crumble at the worst moment. Dollar bills will become useless if the currency falls, so let's keep in mind how vulnerable life is nowadays. But for a farmer, the plantations will become a life saver.

Nomads and starters

Nomads all throughout the deserts tend to stay in nature using the vast land as home. As mentioned before, natural people depend on Mother Nature to sustain life. It's important to keep in mind that our ancestors came from the wilderness at some point back in history. The people of the wilderness usually are safe from all the wars and conflicts.

Indigenous people have a greater chance of avoiding the Islamic rebellions' problems than the people of the city. The Native Americans had a lot of flexibility to live off nature until the Europeans arrived in the 15th century, which changed their whole lives, as more than 75-90% of the North American natives died because of the newcomers. The natives still thrive in South America away from all the trouble.

The caliphate, humanity, and the rest

At some point in the past, all our ancestors came from a natural environment. The city and urban lifestyle have barely advanced to the current supremacy during the last few centuries. Before that, people used animals, such as donkeys and camels, to travel around and needed lots of time to reach far destinations and obtain their needs.

We also have the Eskimo and the Yupik people, who live in the Northern Circumpolar Region, also known as the North Pole Arctic area. Alaska, Greenland and Eastern Siberia are a few examples where natural people still thrive and will stay safer than the troubled cities. The people of the north arctic region are living a natural life, so they have their own way of survival.

Any man and woman will have better chances when having lots of resources to live off, as Mother Nature is very prosperous. Living using the basics of life such as the first humans, who survived living in caves and mud houses, suggests that with the right tools and skills, people can survive, just like the legend Mick Dodge of the American western forests, for example.

Such capabilities and talents are learnable. Shooting guns, bows and arrows, crossbows, riding horses, swimming, and such basic skills are very beneficial when living out in nature. Even country farmers, as mentioned before, will be safer in the case of a social breakdown. But still, the further away people stay from the city, the safer they will be from any social menaces or direct harm that may be caused by the Islamic rebellion and its dangers.

How do societies fall apart?

When a society succeeds and holds power for a long time, it will build a superior society. The longer a nation can stay sufficient and dominate power, the longer it will provide benefits and bring a functional order. Such nations will eventually feel unrivaled and unbeatable. Technological effects and advanced sciences increase this tendency. Over time and after a few generations, the people of the powerful cities might presume that they're untouchable. As generations change, the people will feel that everything will go smoothly. They will become overconfident, which usually leads to failure through arrogant actions followed by disastrous consequences. Technology effects usually influences and cause direct impacts on a nations' confidence.

The caliphate, humanity, and the rest

The caliphate

Social and collective fear, horror, and terror have petrified the people, and the Islamic rebels and jihadists are just one more issue to deal with. There's a lot of war and conflict, and only wisdom and education can defeat it. The world is experiencing tight times because of this matter, and the Middle East political conflicts are increasing the problem. A moral imperative and logical reasoning will solve it. Millions of extreme Muslims and Islamists throughout the world's cities are striving and working on restoring the Muhammadan Caliphate and its socialist Islamic statehood. About one fourth of humanity is Muslim, and some of them are rebelling violently for their cause: to have a global caliphate. This information is not mentioned in order to spread xenophobia, but address and acknowledge what we have in our world.

What can we do? One might ask. A few things would help us to not fall in the trap of the Islamists and jihadists. First of all, we must protect our homeland and keep ourselves safe from any harm that may reach us. Then, we must learn and update our knowledge about the Islamic terrorists, jihadists and rebels, and stay educated about their rebellion. Another necessary step is to strengthen our political and diplomatic relationship with the peaceful Muslims throughout the world who can be a good ally. Finally, we must keep our troops away from harm's way, as interfering in the Middle East militarily will keep dragging us down to the Muhammadan swamp. Let's keep in mind how hardcore Islamists, such as Bin Laden, believe and portray our intervention as a militaristic occupation of their lands.

The caliphate, humanity, and the rest

So humanity is the species of animals that is referred to as the Homo sapiens. Today, Homosapiens live in three types of societies. The most powerful are the ones of the urban areas. The most productive are the ones of the rural areas who are usually farmers and ranchers. And then we have the natural people who still reside in the wilderness.

As mentioned before, Islam is an ideology that originated in the desert. Prophet Muhammad, a bedouin, reformed the monotheist ideology of Abraham the Patriarch and applied it in his statehood: the caliphate. The goal of the Islamic rebellion is to form a global caliphate; Mecca as its capital, and would be a master city to lead the world.

10. The 21st century Middle East issue
Jihadists vs. Zionists

One of our modern global problems is the notoriously disputed city of Jerusalem, which is causing many problems in the Middle East. Not only by the Islamists, but the irredentism by the Zionists in order to re-own Palestine and Greater Israel has been an issue of life and death for the Jewish-Islamic Middle East conflict participants since 1948. Obviously, it's the jihadists' wish to retake the Holy City, as we have learned by now. It's a part of their Islamic liberation and triumph.

Again, we have to understand that there's a section of land on this planet with two groups of people warring over it, and it is affecting billions of people, directly and also indirectly.

The Islamic rebellion was revived by Bin Laden in the 1980s. The Islamic State Caliphate was formed to strengthen the conquest of liberating Jerusalem from the Zionist backed State of Israel.

It's an international issue by now, as the UN considers it a political war, with certain violations on the Israeli side. But still, it seems as if it's been a religious war since day one, not a war over land, policy or governance. Today, it's the jihadists vs. Zionists conflict.

Radicals praise this and blame that

Radicals claim that it's all about Jerusalem. They say that it's all about Jerusalem when actually it's all about them and their actions, but they're ignorant of their doings, and they live in total denial.

Those people who claim that Jerusalem is a holy city are making it sacred for themselves, and if it were not for their claims, then Jerusalem would've never been this infamous. What the people need to understand is that the blame game is a part of living in denial. There is a rebellion in the world, and Jerusalem is a big part of it. All the Abrahamic religions believe that it's a Holy Land, so praising or blaming the other side will not help solve the problem. Each person must look at him or herself and identify how they're involved in this matter, if any at all, and diagnose the matter starting from within.

Caution about the Zionists vs. jihadists conflict

The Jerusalem and Palestine conflict between the Zionists and jihadists has brought new crisis to the entire world. The conflicts' wrath has indirectly reached Europe and North America.

Intentional and accidental massacres by the Zionists and jihadists have taken thousands of lives since the 1920s, and apparently this issue needs to be solved as soon as possible. The blood trails of the Zionist versus jihadist conflict reaches back to the 1920s. Many atrocities have been committed between and by the two sides.

The conflict between the Zionists and jihadists has been here for the last eight decades. Thanks to the cameras and the videos which showed the dramatic scenes all over the world, as we all see how the conflict has been going on our TV screens. Today, the jihad propaganda is all over the world to entice young Muslims to join the rebellion.

All civilized humans know about the Jerusalem conflict. The issue might continue for another decade or two, but inevitably we need to hurry and solve this issue as soon as possible.

The consequences of the turmoil of the Jerusalem problem causes fear and makes the people petrified, and that makes them think that the jihadists will strike with nuclear weapons or atomic bombs in the future. We are in the middle of a crisis, as the Islamic rebellion is in its strongest phase. The world's previous governments obviously failed to solve the terroristic jihad problem, so new governments with newer strategies must be looked for somehow.

We must dismiss the Arab leaders of their duties and call them to resign as soon as possible. Their political problems have spilled everywhere. Their creation of new problems is so intolerable. The Saudi regime, as mentioned before, is a good example of a failing system that is screwing the world right and left.

It's time for new elites to take the lead with new tactics of governance as needed. This is neither a persuasion to deceive our fellow citizens nor an insult to any government or leader. It's a clear reminder, an urgent call, and should be considered as warning about the conflict.

The bottom line

According to the Jews, the Jerusalem dispute is a conflict over soil and land, and that also is the main reason behind the jihadists and Zionists. While there are many religious claims that Jerusalem is a Holy Land, it seems to be creating a lot of mess that brought impurities with the violence that's been happening in that city for the past couple of thousand years. Muslims and Jews aren't causing the problems: it's the Zionists and the jihadists' conflicts.

Although most of the Jews, Christians, or Muslims do not relate biologically to Abraham the patriarch, radical ideologists from those Abrahamic religions have been misusing those creeds to justify their fighting over that land.

Still though, many Jews and Muslims from around the world have entered the clash. Regardless of who owns what, the Islamic rebellion is on, and Jerusalem is what the Islamists are aiming for. The rebels will keep coming out of the dirty south, as Muslim governments are allowing their societies to produce radicals instead of developing moderate human beings with common sense and rational minds.

As long as the dirty south exists, Muslims will keep following the radical jihadists to gain their liberty and obtain their socialist Islamic republic. They learn from previous jihad campaigns, and as long as oppressions and aggression within the Islamic world exists without any visible signs of improvement, the rebellion will go on to expand. There is no other way around it. Young Muslims will rebel and blame their misery on the western world "for stealing their natural resources". They claim that they're not getting a share, as their leaders are taking it all. The Islamists will keep rebelling and jihading until they get a cut. Otherwise, poor and broke imams and preachers will keep sending waves of jihadists and rebels in the cause of the holy jihad.

Also, regardless of the Islamic jihadi duty to fight or liberate Jerusalem, as long as the irredentism of the Zionists and negligence of the American politicians goes on, young and mad Muslims will continue to rebel against imperialism, crony capitalism and anti-Islamic tendencies. For now, the caliphate is back in effect, and for the average American, combating the Islamists or the Islamic State Caliphate (ISC) is not an obligation. For the average American, combating the jihadists is merely optional, so our involvement in war against them is not essential.

Capitalism and ownership

Capitalism provides the right to property, but from the natural perspective, there's no such thing as ownership of the land because land belongs to all. The city people claim lands as assets and promote personal rights of ownership. The UN allows dividing the land and permits governments to take land as their property, which today is one of the core problems within mankind civilization. The UN allows nations to have the right to an area, form armies, place their own laws and rule the land as they wish. Although it is accepted by most humans today, land ownership creates conflicts and wars.

As the world is divided into nations and countries, it separates the people and creates divisions. That's where jealousy, envy and animosity develop to cause problems between the rich and poor. For example, Jerusalem is the most important city that the UN should worry about and fix its problem before it brings World War III onto humanity. The United States of America, as the current superpower, should deal with this issue positively as soon as possible.

Fear!

In order for us to solve the problem, we must not be terrified of the situation and face it head on. Fear is the worst mental emotion that people and other beings could experience. Harm, violence, conflicts and war are a source of fear, and there are times where people live in constant personal fear and social tensions. Today, many parties use fear to control the masses.

Fear is the most effective factor that overwhelms people and causes them to be subdued easily. Fear on social levels can be seen with law-abiding masses that fear the consequences of breaking the law. Punitive action for breaking the laws of any land in any civil society forces the people to obey the law that they're born into. Fear, as we see today, became a tool that people use to bring control on others. When we see people abiding the law and driving down the street according to the speed limit, let it be recognized that people are worried about their safety but also are afraid of getting a speeding violation ticket.

Crime is another source of fear. Fear, as we see today, has engulfed cities, as criminals such as thieves, robbers and bandits target innocent individuals and civilians. Fear, as we see today in human civilization, has torn us apart, as people stopped trusting others with many things. That's why we lock our doors at night.

But, we need to come out of our fears and confront it head on. Remember, "the only thing we have to fear is fear itself", as Franklin Roosevelt said.

The 21st century Middle East issue

Cities and the fear factor

The more corrupt rulers are, the more they favor controlling their people by having them live in cities and close proximities. The more corrupted rulers are, the more they tend to use physical force against their civilians. Today, many Muslims who reside in the Old World are still being terrorized from living like other average humans because they know that severe punishment could come at any minute if they oppose their governments or regimes. The Iranian government, for example, executes convicts publicly. Not just malicious governments do such things, but even gangs and mobs kill to inject fear. Look what the drug cartels in Mexico do to gain power.

Interlinked areas and cities with roads and highways provide easier control of the civilians and masses. Connected by roads, city structures help today's governments rule the people, and that's why the cities' governments are superior and have control over the land while the UN sometimes approves and sometimes denounces their actions.

Fear controls the masses

For thousands of years, many governments have used fear as a tool to control the masses. President John Adams expressed that "fear is the foundation of most governments." Until this day, many governments are still using the same tool of fear to control the masses. Urban cities and civil societies enable governments to gain central power. Rural areas and desolate lands disable total control by the governments. Another example of social fear is the civilians and how the pay taxes imposed by the governments to avoid punishment.

Even natural disasters spread social fear, as many people prepare and take precautions for such problems nowadays. Today, many fear nature's forces, such as tornados, tsunamis, and earthquakes.

Terrorists play another factor of social fear. The city residents of the Red Nations taste some of the jihadists' terror once in a while. Some claim that it's God's wrath, but it's also a human-made terror, which could be solved by humans as well. Living in cities always brings fear and horror upon people, more than those of the non-urban areas.

As of today, religious persecution is another cause of social fear, as Jews suffered it in the Holocaust; Muslims experienced it in the Mongols invasions, and Christians endured it during the times of Jesus

Christ. Africans in the Congo have faced this problem; Armenians suffered it during World War I, and many minorities in Iraq are facing this problem today as well.

Fear and horror forces the people to live in constant fright which is totally unhealthy. Terror does control the people, but people usually end up uniting and breaking all the evil that brings horror unto a nation. Sooner or later, the problem of fear will be solved, but our efforts need to be put in place as soon as possible. We must not be afraid or petrified of any evil.

Fear of governments is a problem that's increasing, as master cities usually spread their power and influence on others of other cities and locations. It is important that we must come out of our fears and take any problem head on. Many corrupted parties use fear to control the civilian masses, and that's why it's necessary for us to make sure that we're bold and brave, instead of being timid and meek.

Misled by fear

President George W. Bush stated that Operation Iraqi Freedom would free the Iraqis, and he later claimed that the mission had been accomplished. The interpretation of freedom, as Operation Iraqi Freedom displayed, is very misleading. But its fear that got us there.

President George H. Bush provoked Bin Laden in the 1990s, and so Bin Laden declared war on America as payback for the intervention in the Muslim world's problems. We can conclude that the actions of his son, President George W. Bush, enabled Al-Baghdadi II to gain power and seize vast lands in the Middle East by establishing the Islamic State of Iraq and Syria which enabled him to revive the caliphate.

Warning of World War III aka Armageddon

Inequality increases social division, which eventually ignites collective conflicts and wars. The war against jihad isn't a simple matter, as we have learned, where many disasters could follow. The inequality in the Middle East is creating the final generation of fighters, as the Islamic State Caliphate claims today.

We, the Americans, need to find a quick solution for all the aggression before it's too late. If we stay involved militarily in the Middle Eastern problems, Armageddon could hit home and might even reach our homeland and cities like the events of 9/11. So we must be rational.

The 21st century Middle East issue

Many parts of the Middle East still have a chance to be saved. By now it's too late for Syria. Saudi Arabia could fall next, just like Iraq did. Islam, in general, promotes equality, and Saudi Arabia doesn't provide equality. That causes the young Saudi youth to fall for the radical imams that turn them into Islamic rebels, who create all the madness that some nations are experiencing. Osama Bin Laden was a Saudi youth at some point in the past, and neglecting him at that time permitted him to go on full blast and wage the war that he did. So education is the key to success.

Fear within the world' community is very visible. Because of the Islamic prophecies, the current caliphate (ISC) believes that it will fight on the eastern side of Armageddon, as Israel and its allies will come from the west. The ISC is trying to indicate that it has the last mass and group of devoted jihadists that are supposed to reach Jerusalem and fight the final battle of Armageddon. According to the biblical revelation, eventually, a 200-million man army will march and enter the Holy Lands and raise Armageddon, and might end up murdering a 3rd of mankind in its war campaign. It seems as if the Islamic State Caliphate is gathering that army, and temple mount is their primary destination. But either way, the current jihadists will make the last wave of warriors of Islam, who could wage the next world war possibly within the next 30 years. Now that's a long-term project, and if the poverty and injustice levels of the Islamic world do not improve, millions of young Muslims can and will be recruited by the jihadists and other rebels to enter their jihad campaign. On the internet, we found two interesting but controversial articles that discussed the revelation. The first was written by Walid Shoebat and can be found at   www.shoebat.com/2014/09/25/every-christian-needs-know-200-million-man-army-will-march-israel/
The second article was written by Monica Dennington and can be found at   www.tictocministries.wordpress.com/2014/10/27/isis-prophecy-the-200-million-man-army-2/

The Saudi Arabian royal family is a close ally of the United States, but the Saudi people are sick of the ill-treatment by the Saudi-American backed government and may revolt at any time, just as Bin Laden's group did. The democracy of America effects Saudi Arabia, and the Saudi people understand how it works and the youth are at risk. The next few quatrains will explain how.

The 21st century Middle East issue

America provides liberty. Saudi Arabia provides constraint

Saudi women live under very strict rules and regulations. The Saudi regime tries to keep women at a low profile, as Islam supposedly described. Leaving Islam is punishable by death, so there's no such thing as individual independence for the Saudi people. The main question now is: why didn't President George W. Bush free the Saudi people from the autocracy they're living under?

In Saudi Arabia driving for women is prohibited, traveling alone is disliked, and supporting women's rights is unfavorable. All that causes desperation within the Saudi people, as families could be doing better without those restrictions. Even though Saudi Arabia has about quarter of a trillion barrels of oil reserves, poverty rates are up to 20%.

America provides public liberty. Saudi Arabia provides social restraint

By voting and engaging in the political process, the American civilians enjoy the right to choose and elect the government officials. The American people were never as restrained as the Saudi Arabian people are, and that's why the majority of Saudis are sick of the current tyrannical monarchy! Monarchies are dictatorships within Islam, where Islam recommends the people to elect their leaders by political voting and selection. That does not exist in the Kingdom of Saudi Arabia, as most of the Saudis have been calling and some are revolting for a change.

The power in America, as we know, is held by many parties. Many in America enjoy their freedom by joining interest groups and political parties. America is a pluralist democracy, as the people are represented by the parties they elect, where such a democratic system doesn't exist in Saudi Arabia. In Saudi Arabia, the monarch rules all he wants, regardless of what the outcomes are. There's no democracy in Saudi Arabia, and that also adds fuel to the fire.

Some Muslims claim that opposing dictatorship and combating tyranny, such as the current regime of Saudi Arabia, is considered to be a high jihadic duty. It is supposed to be honored by Islam, where some Muslims even claim that rebelling against cruel and malicious governments is a great cause to fight for and that resisting a tyrant is the same as serving God. Bin Laden actually followed such Islamic duty, as the concept of jihading against tyrants is increasing rapidly within the Islamic world. Even Hitler addressed how Islam praises such actions, so it's pretty understandable why Muslims steadily rebel and commit jihad. And let's make it clear, there are almost no complete democracies within most of the Islamic world. Saudi Arabia is totally authoritarian. Even Islamic democracy does not exist in that country such as other Islamic nations as the UAE, Jordan, Afghanistan, Bahrain, Morocco, Kuwait, etc. Such authoritarianism, such as of Saudi Arabia's, is the main producer of Islamic rebelling, terrorism and jihadism. That's why Islamic preachers and imams are gaining the upper hand and were able to produce the current rebelling younger generations. The current caliphate (ISC) is also playing a big role in producing jihad today, let's keep that in mind.

Are the next 20 American presidents going to leave Saudi Arabia like the way it is and shake hands with its monarchs and do Arab dances as well? President George W. Bush danced with the leader of a country that produced 15 out of the nineteen 9/11 attackers, how does that work?

Arabian kings and princes

1. The Kingdom of Saudi Arabia – There are only two older brothers left in the succession of the King Saud dynasty inheritance. As soon King Salman and his crown prince dies, the country will have a power struggle because of a feud between the third generation princes. It is very possible that the issue is going to provoke a physical conflict and a civil war. Iran is going to try to move in by supporting and supplying Shiite militants and terrorists. If a civil war kicks off, other parties will try to take advantage of the situation as well. The Islamic State Caliphate is working hard on the issue right now, and there are thousands of young Saudis and sleeper cells are in support of the caliphate against the Saud dynasty.

2. Jordan – Two-thirds of Jordan's residents are non-Jordanians. About 40% of the Jordanian population is from a Palestinian decent who fled the Arab-Israeli wars. The Jordanian monarch is in a very sensitive situation, as more than half of the Jordanian population lives under the poverty level. Most native Jordanians are bedouins who fell in a social breakdown since the 1967 war. Many Jordanian youth are on the edge of jihading and rebelling. The people of Jordan should seek safety, so they might as well pick up their wealth and flee the area since it might get hectic within the next three decades. Muammar Al-Gaddafi of Libya and the way that his people backstabbed him is a good example of such threatening dilemmas for the Jordanian leadership and monarchy.

3. Bahrain – The Bahraini Monarch should be embarrassed of himself. Lots of his people hate him, as he is a dictator, and his country might fall very quickly into the control of Iran. Thousands of Bahrainis are waiting for a total revolution to hit home. The Bahraini people are steadily readying themselves to revolt against the dictatorship regime. Bahrain is in jeopardy. The best advice for the king of Bahrain is to move to Europe before he loses the chance to be saved, God forbid.

4. Morocco – The day Morocco collapses and falls into the grip of the Islamic State, the Moroccan King and his regime will be overthrown. Again, the best choice for Morocco is a constitutional republic. Other than that, the Moroccan people will continue to struggle, and it will end up as a failed state sooner or later and might fall into the grip of the caliphate or other militants someday.

Many more Arabs

The Islamic rebellion might reach further than expected. Fifteen years ago, no Iraqi saw it coming. Persecuting Muslims increases the problem, and will always reflect back and enlarge the support for the Islamic rebellion. Provoking Muslims will strengthen the Islamic rebellion, and it will gain power and strike harder throughout the world in the future. Obviously, there are some sick Muslims who are willing to commit violent – suicidal jihad, and that's why we're ought to careful about dealing with them.

The Islamic rebellion and its influences have flooded Mesopotamia, Babylon, North Africa and Central Asia. Tunisia, Algeria, Egypt, Yemen and West Asia are at great risk, as millions of Muslims seem to be willing to follow the active rebels of the Islamic cause in support of a caliphate regime.

The majority of Arabs are Sunni Muslims, who have been quiet and peaceful for the most part. Many of them started rebelling and revolting against the world since the jihading and Islamic rebellion was revived by Bin Laden. The revolutions were taking place one at a time, but the Arab Spring opened the door for the Islamic rebellion to expand its grip on the politics of the Middle East and Islamic world. Unfortunately, the sleeping Sunni giant has woken up. By now, we have more than 1.7 billion Muslims; most are peaceful but some may rebel at any time they get the patience squeezed out of them. Jihadism has become a spread-out phenomenon throughout the world nowadays.

Reaching the rest of the world

City residents are usually in danger more than their government officials. The residents are at more risk than their rulers, so they should take precautions personally. The Paris attacks of 2015 affirm this detail.

The people of every city should realize and keep note of their actions and identify the risks of the consequences that their governments are putting them through. The residents of every nation should not wait to be bombed with a dirty bomb, a nuclear device or other harmful weapons and objects. Instead, they need to choose better options that will save lives better than staying ignorant and adding risks to the problem. In 2015, a Russian airliner full of civilians was bombed over Egypt as a result of the Russian government's intervention in the Middle East. This type of problem is what the civilians need to be aware of.

Cautions for the religious

Buddha taught about self-restraint and recommended to hold a highly moral conduct when dealing with others. Taming the mind, tongue, and actions are basics that every Buddhist can't ignore; otherwise they will be out of the faith of Buddha.

Judaism as well prohibits killing and murdering others. Bloodshed is against Judaism, and anyone who violates is out of Judaism and is rebelling against the concept of Jewish faith.

Jesus Christ advised to love the enemy and hate no one. For the person should forgive the inexcusable actions of others, in order for the Lord to forgive their inexcusable actions and thoughts.

The Quran states not to kill innocent lives. Muhammad gave orders against revenge, so when a Muslim commits any act of revenge those orders are broken. Any Muslim who commits revenge has drifted off the Muhammadan rules and regulations.

Many guilty individuals have embarrassed their religions and faiths, and some humans took the name of the Lord in vain, as they created for themselves a bad image among humanity. This is dangerous because it involves billions of people and their values about life. As Jesus Christ taught, people can be recognized by their fruits. It's not what goes into the mouth that defines the man; it's what comes out the mouth that defines a man. A good man will bring good things out of the good that's stored in him, and an evil man will bring bad things out of the wickedness that's been growing in him. Check the fruits, identify the healthy ones and pick them as leaders from the sickened ones.

While some devout Christians believe that they're the final generation of God, Muhammad is a name that is steadily being brought up in America. Obviously, the Muhammadan swamp has infiltrated.

Keep in mind that George Washington was the main physical founding father of America. But now, America is need of a new mental father, as Christ's system is collapsing. Atheism in America is on the rise, Churches are losing followers rapidly, other religions are growing faster, etc. The billionaire businessman Donald Trump has acted as if he's there to save America and Christianity. Whether he's telling truth or not isn't the case. We, the civilians, can and should stand up and care for our religious beliefs, but must care for our national union first.

The same for the Islamic rebels and jihadists

Killing will never bring permanent freedom, but enjoying a good meal, having a lovely family and earning legitimate income is the way to do it. Not all Muslims have those goods in their life, and fighting wars might not necessarily bring joy or happiness. It's all a part of the human struggle while some people are fighting to get rich and some die trying.

We're in the 21st century, and humans still invade and hurt each other like wild animals, and it's been recorded that it has been going on for the past 8,000 years. That's when the first collective conflicts started taking place, and since then, wars have been documented to occur more often. Muslims are rebelling in the thousands, and that's why we see lots of wars in the Middle East, and that's their method of gaining the Islamic liberation and freedom. Muslims are turning from average civilians into warriors that go out there and commit acts of violence to bring victory to their side. Again, it's all human error and could be solved.

Imams vs. American Republicans

Hillary Clinton says, "What's wrong with the Republicans? Do they hate the Muslims?"

Some claim that the far right Republicans are the ones who misuse America for their wants and placed us in front of the jihadists' wrath. As we mentioned before, Bin Laden never went to war with America until President George H. Bush sent the American troops to

The 21st century Middle East issue

Saudi Arabia during the Gulf war, which raised lots of emotions throughout the Middle East. His son got us involved in another Iraq war in 2003 named Operation Iraqi Freedom. Well, all the dictatorships must be replaced, not just in Iraq. Iran has been another main cause of the Islamic terrorism. Today, some feel that the Iraq war was over oil. Regardless, the Iraq war has woken up the sleeping Sunni giant.

By now, the war is more looking like if it's Islamic jihadism versus America. Just six decades ago, it was only the Zionists versus the Islamic imams' conflict. By n ow, the war of the two ideologies has turned into a full-scale open-ended war on America, waged by those jihadists and Islamic imams and their rebelling followers. But the war evolved eventually, and now we have the Red Nations versus the Islamic State Caliphate war, as the radical imams aren't giving up at all.

The current caliphate (ISC)

The caliphate is the Islamic statehood, which is the governing body led by the grand imam. As mentioned before, the former Ottoman Caliphate was abolished back in 1924, and that's what the Islamic rebels reestablished in June 2014. The Islamic State Caliphate, as mentioned before, runs upon the doctrine of Prophet Muhammad's caliphate and the succession of his political system. Ultimately, the caliphate is what the devout, extreme and radical Muslims are seeking to form.

Israel – in the middle of it

Israel is located in the heart of the Islamic world, which the Islamists are trying to wipe out by any means. Liberating Palestine and Jerusalem is one of the Islamic rebellion's main goals.

Other than that, the caliphate has been revived, and by now, it controls territories all over the Middle East and Islamic world, from Algeria to Afghanistan. The current caliphate's capital is Al-Raqqah, which is located on the Euphrates River in the heart of Mesopotamia.

The current caliphate has many other Islamic states throughout the Old World. The Islamic State Caliphate has set its main goal, which includes regaining Jerusalem from the grip of the Zionists.

America, the powerful

America is queen bee of the world. Even though the American people make up only 5% of the world's population, the political, financial and military power of the United State makes it the dominant country in the world. If America is polluted, then the world has no other savior and mischief will continue. Every conscious American should keep that in mind and therefor assist America. If not, the jihadists will feed on America's weakness. America is the source of justice and after America, there won't be complete justice.

Is terrorism the war of the poor?

Humanity is living a totally unjust life, where the rich keep getting richer and the poor keep suffering more and more, every day, even though it is unfair. These conditions could result in the failing of our civil society. They will push the people to rebel, like the Watts Riots of L.A. in 1965. People will continue to resist and fend off oppression, and one day, the poor will be fed up and revolt eventually. That's what the Islamic rebellion is all about. The reason Al-Baghdadi II was able to put the caliphate of the Islamic State together was because of the backup that he received from starving Iraqis and Syrians, who were full of it and had had enough with President Assad of Syria and Mr. Al-Maliki, the former leader of Iraq. Both the Syrian and Iraqi people protested and tried to bring attention to their case during the 2011 Arab Spring. With the help of Abu Bakr Al-Baghdadi, the jihadists were able to combine the lands and abolish the Iraqi-Syrian border. Using Muhammad's prophetic doctrine, Al-Baghdadi II created the new Islamic caliphate in June 2014. Then, some Iraqi and Syrian people got what they wanted: an Islamic State. We have billions of people around the world who are still struggling and living in poverty even though they display high levels of self-control and holding back from revolting and creating chaos. As mentioned before, most of the Saudi people are demonstrating highly disciplined behavior and peaceful approaches. The same goes for the American people; most are still behaving correctly.

In the next quatrain, we'll look at some recent peaceful approaches by the public, though the whole situation could escalate and become more aggressive if left neglected for the next few decades.

Occupy everything

The new generations feel that they are the 99% of the population who are less fortunate and wish to replace the current misery by protesting. But without having purified leadership, it will be hard to accomplish by simply having poor people protest and show their united presence. That's why Senator Bernie Sanders received lots of support during the 2016 election cycle as he promoted a socialist America for all.

That's where the Islamic rebellion originates, starting with some depressed and oppressed individuals who resist oppression and want to form a socialist Islamic nation that cares for its followers. During the 20th century, it was Bin Laden who led the fight against what he called the "evil axis and tyrant dictators" as he went on following Prophet Muhammad's model of rebelling.

Muhammad and the 99%

As mentioned before, Muhammad was an orphan who came to a world full of fuss and misery. He dealt with the issue by standing up to lead a prophetic movement of destitute rebels against the rich. As Bin Laden displayed, Muslims nowadays are rebelling against the capitalism of the west. Keep in mind that most Muslims live in the dirty south's poverty, which also raises the tensions. Prophet Muhammad's calls to perform charity and paying alms came with his message of monotheism, as he claimed that donations cleanse the sin. We explained before how he learned such practices from the Judaism's Tzedakah. He also created the caliphate, which introduced the socialist Islamic caliphate, where the poor received welfare and were cared for by authority. We have found an interesting article written by Danios regarding Prophet Muhammad and the 99% movement. For more information, please go online and visit www.loonwatch.com/2012/02/muhammad-is-the-99-percent/

Last advice

Every individual must stay aware and alert of what's taking place around him or her. For the social, economic and security matters, each civilian carries the duty of caring for him or herself. As mentioned before, it is very critical to keep aware of our direct surroundings as well.

A citizen must also care for his local community and whole society. As mentioned before, if there are violent people or aggressors, from thieves to terrorists, one must protect him or herself from any danger that's ahead. Whether it's Islamists or lone wolves; sick, mad or violent Muslims, they can be viewed as potential terrorists, and so we must stay aware. But one must avoid provocative actions toward them, and in the case of emergencies, contacting the authorities is important, though most Islamists practice self-discipline anyways.

The 21st century Middle East issue

Again, it is not an obligation for any civilian to oppose or combat the Islamic rebels, thus it is the duty of the whole world community, led by the United States of America as a reliable power, to solve this problem that originates from the Islamic world and specifically the Middle East. Electing better leaders and officials is the citizens' duty at all times. Concerning Islamic terrorism, jihadism and rebelling, learning and gaining intellectual education may be very beneficial; just like this warning which informs about the Islamic rebellion.

By the law

Victory can be gained. By voting and electing righteous men, we the people will produce and enjoy a great future. Peace can be obtained politically at all times.

America is the mother of justice. If the current world order is damaging America, then we the people are obligated to fix the crisis. The governing system needs to operate perfectly in order for the future to be better. There will be no justice after America, so our nation's wellness is paramount.

Warning

The global economy is at risk. The global market system is in danger for the simple fact that our civilization is becoming unstable with its social, financial and political issues. The possibility of World War III occurring in the 21st century is very high. The population of the world is growing rapidly, while hope is running low.

Equality brings peace. Equality is what humanity needs by now. Not only sick-of-life Arabs and young Muslims are at risk, but the current cold war between America and communism is also a threat to the world. Communism is threatening America, which is also menacing to the world, and it certainly needs to be terminated as soon as possible. Iran, Venezuela, North Korea, Cuba, Brazil, India, China, Russia and such systems from the communist bodies are also causing sickness in the world, along with the devious envy that communists shoot toward America. If the Ottoman Empire was the sick man of Europe during the 19th century, today we have some sick communists that replaced it.

Einstein's "World War IV with sticks and stones" theory could become a reality. War is never an answer and can never solve problems permanently. For the problems of the Islamic world, education and political diplomacy is the only way to fix them.

Doomsday possibility in the near future is very high. The people need to learn a few more things. The Israelis should care for themselves and dig and prepare long-lasting bunkers, not just temporary shelters, if they wish to stay in Israel because Armageddon is verily forthcoming. If the conflict reaches such levels, vehicle mobility will be disabled; as food and main necessities won't make it far from farms.

Preparations for emergencies are never a loss. Learning how to be self-sufficient is always a plus. Plantations, cultivation, farming, raising livestock, hunting and fishing will always be there for mankind. Domestic animals are always a good source of survival, if our civilization fails or collapse.

As of February 2015, it became clear that Jordan is in a long-term war with the Islamic State Caliphate. The Jordanian Monarch called it World War III, as the Islamic State Caliphate is looking at Jordan as the next neighborhood for the Islamic annexation to recruit it to the union of the Islamic States. This might cause more instability in the region in the long run, as Jordan has lots of Islamists and sleeper cells. Algeria is facing the same dilemma as well.

The same way Bin Laden was a sleeper rebel when he was a young boy; many people in the Middle East are being born into the assembly line of jihadism. But that's not the problem in this case. The perspective of the young and buck-wild Muslims who strike anywhere they can reach is a sobering reality for the Red Nations.

Most young Muslims are eager to gain wealth and status; even though they're born into poverty under tyrannies and dictatorships. Many autocrats, such as the Saudi monarch, still control the Muslim masses, which limits the capacities of the Muslim youth to earn their needs. That's why we have this influx of Muslims that are rebelling and jihading. Poverty due to the social injustice in the Islamic world is the core of the problem, and the Islamic State Caliphate is exploiting on it.

Muslims fast for Ramadan every year, which makes Muslims compassionate for other Muslims who are starving and have little to live off of. Their fellow weak and poor Muslims don't need the rebellion, but the rebellion is built on such divisions among them. That's what keeps the Islamic rebellion on the move every time an imam reminds fellow

Muslims about their case and cause, which is to liberate the Islamic world and establish a socialist Islamic empire.

Common sense, not war

Even though 99% of the American army officers and officials are loyal to the United State, terror can even hit from inside the military ranks. The Fort Hood shooting by Sergeant Nidal Hasan is an excellent example of such cracks in the system.

Obviously, not every soldier is a standup guy. Some are loyal to the United States but some fight for the money, benefits and pension.

Unless someone takes America by the hand and pulls it out of the grip of aggression, the role will stay filled by ineffective leaderships and weak cabinets who care less about the people and care more about themselves, as we have witnessed since the 1960s. Since the 1960s, it is the American people who raised this country, not the government!

Reminders

Concerning the American radicalized Muslims, The FBI director Comey said it's as if they have "a devil sitting on their shoulder saying 'Kill, Kill, Kill, Kill, all day long...." Do you think that's true?

Humans are very intellectual and enjoy very high perception levels. People need to be taught morality instead of barbarianism. Free men and women do not transgress, regardless of others' attitudes, feelings and thoughts toward them. Morality always wins, slowly but steadily. We need to stay as pure as possible to hold our peace of mind.

Humans are stuck on this planet, and that has led some to feel confused and out of place. Humans have lost their role of mastering the universe, even though we are the most intellectual beings on Earth.

Free citizens trust their tacit knowledge and don't rely on weirdos to lead their way, such as electing celebrities and actors to be leaders for example. Free men and women enjoy their instinct, conscience and 6th sense, instead of following behind the blind masses who are deceived by the comfort of the urban life.

The civilians need to be mindful and elegant, not loose and rubbish. Free men and women take the lead, instead of following a crowd of misguided and confused people.

Our civilization has to exercise openness and show acceptance to others. Acceptance and openness are the key to victory, and education is vital to defeat evil within our world.

But for the Islamic rebellion, it is in effect. The Islamic rebellion is aiming its horror on the Red Nations. Until those nations and their people find and make peace with the Islamic world, the Islamic rebellion will send warriors to harm them, as Prophet Muhammad will stay their number one idol and his rebellious ideology will keep finding many followers and adherents to retain the rebellion proceeding.

Looking at the bigger picture

By looking at the big picture, it's obvious that the combination of events over the past 4,000 years resulted in the current Islamic rebellion. As long the State of Israel does not call peace with the Arab Muslims and simply allow Muslims to the right of Palestine and Holy Land, the Islamic rebellion will go on, and millions of Muslims will come and dedicate themselves to the Islamic liberation and jihadi cause. Poverty and injustice throughout the Islamic world will increase the lethality of the Islamic rebellion. The monarch of Jordan has warned of this issue before.

President George W. Bush didn't introduce democracy to the Saudi people, who still suffer from the problems of the Islamic rebellion. The Saudis are steadily losing their boys, who rebel and get involved personally in the war of the Islamic rebellion and its jihadism. President George W. Bush should've been reminded that it was not Weapons of Mass Destruction that struck America on 9/11; it was a bunch of Saudis who used their bodies to operate jumbo jets and flew them into their targets. President Bush's words about Saddam Hussein, terrorists, and WMDs petrified the American people. But he left the Saudi tyranny alone, which can be seen as a double standard to many people.

Today, somewhere in Saudi Arabia, some young men could be in the process of being raised to become the next attackers of America, just like the 15 Saudis out of the 19 men that hijacked the airplanes and attacked NYC and the pentagon on 9/11. Even though it was claimed that Saddam Hussein was connected to the 9/11 attack; other than his hostile attitude, he actually had nothing to do with it. It was the Saudi regime that should've been taken out of office for its continuous growth of radical Islamists, rebels and terrorists. As far as we know, Saddam Hussein has never detonated a bomb on any American land or flown airplanes into any American city towers, nor will he ever. But still, many Arabs saw Saddam Hussein as a hero who was actually another Islamic rebel that carried on his duty and became an icon in combating their opposition by fighting for the Arabic dream. Saddam Hussein was only conducting a psychological warfare and presented himself as another Hitler, even though he didn't get that close to any global dominance at all. And today, other Arabs are willing to carry on the movement.

The final prophecy

Abraham the Patriarch, the nomad from Iraq, initiated the rebellious religious ideology. Moses remodeled it, Muhammad reformed it, and Bin Laden revived another cycle of it. All Bin Laden did is use the Muhammadan rebellious philosophy to conduct his jihadi project.

Osama Bin Laden was the main Sunni Arab who retriggered the influx of the Islamic rebellion and confirmed the aims of the global jihad by the beginning of the 21st century.

The Zionist – jihadist dispute has nothing to do with the United States of America. Until the American contribution to foreign wars ceases and America stops intervening militarily in the raging wars and conflicts within the Islamic world, the rebels and jihadists will keep attacking America and targeting its allies. Only diplomacy will solve it.

Here's the fictional irony that Abrahamites have their faith in: according to the Muslims, a man will come and call a truce between the Abrahamites and guide them to what's right, and they call him the Mahdi. Mahmoud Ahmadinejad, the former leader of Iran, has boasted about that before. On the same hand, the Jews are waiting for their Moshiach (Messiah), the Israelite Tzadik, as they're still fighting over Jerusalem and its surroundings, which is claimed to be his homeland. Christians are also awaiting their Messiah, Jesus Christ, to come and save the world. Till then, today's Islamic rebellion by the worldly imams against Israel and its allies goes on. The terror might just go on until the last Islamist, jihadist, and Islamic rebel dies in this war. This struggle has been going on for the past four thousand years.

Sincerely

It's very fair to conclude that given the prophetic philosophy produced after the monotheist Abraham, which is taught by its many faces and sides by the prophets, with the current availability of efficient weapons and firearms, and combined with the poverty and negligence of the dirty south, the Islamic rebellion will continue and may last for tens, if not hundreds of years. What we have is a mass of extremely mad Muslims and radical Islamists that will rebel and jihad against every society, regardless of the existence of the caliphate, Iran, Saudi Arabia or not. There's a high likelihood of Muslims jihading and taking all kinds of actions to strike back and rebel against whomever stand in their way until the end. Whether they do it for envying Islam's flourished rivals or for being under the control of tyrants and dictators, they will rebel to gain a better life and future. The troubling situation makes the Muslims assume and think they're under a Judeo-Christian conspiracy that's being carried to annihilate them.

The urban versus rural effects also add to the problem as most Muslims live in the Old World. Again, most Islamic rebels are the victims of unjust societies. Whether the people of the Middle East are Muslims or not they all need democracy and tranquility in their life. Plus, a decent life and a comfortable existence always makes people happier and will result in fewer reasons for the people to rebel and go against the grain. The Arab Spring enabled Al-Baghdadi II to annex whatever the rebels conquered in Syria, and that enabled him to revive the Islamic caliphate in 2014. Wrongful wars and arrogant actions by the Western leaders have helped the jihadists rebuild the caliphate.

Russia, Saudi Arabia or Turkey won't solve the problem. The international community led by the United Sates is the only party that can fix the problem and bring peace to the world. As a matter of a fact, the tyranny of the leaders of the Islamic world adds fuel to the fire, instead of killing the burning lake as they're allowing it to spill over and reach other communities. The calls, instructions and propaganda of the jihadists have already flooded the world and are gaining fans every day.

The international ignorance of the Jerusalem conflict, the constant wars against the wrong parties along the arrogant decisions by the lawmakers keeps the Islamic rebelling movement's flaming fire to continue. Young and eager Middle Easterners will keep forming nationalist groups such as the Baath Arabic party, Islamist groups such as Al-Qaeda and patriotic groups such as the Palestinian Liberation Organization (PLO) to achieve their goals and desires. Poverty and lack of social justice will intensify the problem.

The Islamic rebellion

As the keyword in rebellions is freedom, some devout and many mad Muslims are sick of the injustice that enslaved their lands and lives, and today, they are rebelling and revolting for the sake of their Islamic socialism. They want to gain the Islamic liberation and establish their Muhammadan polity, which would be an absolute Islamic empire that would consist of one-fourth of the world's population. This type of revolutions by the Middle Easterners has been occurring for thousands of years, and their actions stand for the common phrase "give me liberty, or give me death," and they are carrying it all the way. Keep in mind that they're still humans, so it's up to us whether we solve the matter or not.

The Islamic rebellion is taking place in our planet. Many Muslims may not realize that they're a part of the overall Islamic rebellion even though the bigger picture of what is taking place is pretty understandable. Mr. Donald Trump said, "There is something going in mosques…." Yes, it's the Islamic rebellion. Simply, it's because the imams teach to follow and abide by the Quran which is the heart of the Islamic jihadism. A person might think this is a lie, but it's not. If one wants a proof, he should attend the Friday sermons for a year or two, along with the night sessions and observe how the Muslims are uniting and striving hard; just as the followers of Prophet Muhammad did back in the early 600s. Now, of course not every outsider would notice this, but actually it is an Islamic rebellion that is being produced by the imams and preachers throughout the Islamic world. Mr. Donald Trump said, "We are at *war* with *radical Islamic terrorists*." Sure, that could be the case, but we're also at *war vs. the Islamic rebellion.*

The Shiite Muslims are actively engaging in debates and discussions about the Islamic rebellion as Ayatu-Allah Kumaini admitted that he's a major figure in the rebellion back in the 1970s. They believe that their future leader is the hidden 12th imam, better known as the Mahdi, who is supposed to be arriving soon and will lead them to victory. That's why many radical Shiites have been forming groups and militias as they wait for him to come and lead their way. The *Mahdi army*, which became popular after the 2003 Iraq war, is the best example. But most Muslims, in general, are not aware that they're a part of the rebellion. One may wonder how could that be possible, but it's easy to understand.

During the European Renaissance, from Italy to France, Germany and Britain most Christians were busy focused on their own business and striving for the best. The Europeans were gaining education in mathematics, biology, geography, cosmology, philosophy, theology, history, arts, architecture, medical studies and more. They were not aware that they were conducting a massive European revolution, the Renaissance, as they were busy working every day. In the same sense, the Muslims around the world are doing about the same thing, which is raising an Islamic rebellion without noticing it. Most Muslims are very peaceful, while some others are very hostile. Ultimately, they're paving the way for each other to gain power and dominance over what they see as God's will and compensation to his people. From the peaceful to the violent Muslims, most of them actually do follow the same Muhammadan rebellious philosophy which is instructed in the Quran. Osama Bin Laden, as we speculate, was the 1st of the 12 imams who will conclude the Islamic rebellion. The book's back cover shows what the line of imams may be like, which could lead to the 12th hidden imam, the Mahdi, as described in the Islamic prophetic apocalypses.

Rationally

All the prophetic, biblical and apocalyptic accounts aside; we can be very rational about the situation. Let's not be hypocritical about this issue. At the end of the day, the Zionist versus jihadi conflict causes the Islamic rebellion to grow in strength and power. As of 2016, seven decades after the establishment of Israel, the war is still going as the Islamists are rebelling and jihading. Those disputes along with the tyrannical governments of the Islamic world are the central cause for the Islamic rebellion. Saudi Arabia is the main producer of suicide jihad.

It can be a 40-year struggle if dealt with correctly, or it may become a 1000-year war; if left neglected. Until the end, this *warning* about the *war versus the Islamic rebellion* will be a tool to guide those who are trying to gain some knowledge about the current jihadism. It's a mini guidebook for those who are trying to figure out what is going on with the terrorists and their conflict. Meanwhile, the war with the Islamic rebels goes on in many parts of the world, even at this moment.

ABOUT THE AUTHOR

My biography will be placed in the 4th letter of the warning, which is NAME: 21st CENTURY CIVILIAN. Anyways, let me share the reason why I have brought forth *war vs. the Islamic rebellion.*

As a Sunni Arab who grew up in the Middle East, I never understood the Islamic jihadism cause until the year 2014. Growing up in the Middle East and then migrating to America in 2001 enabled me to explore the jihadism reality from both sides, as an American civilian and also as a Muslim Arab. Before the 9/11 attacks, I have heard of Osama Bin Laden, but I never really understood why he was deemed as a hero within the Islamic world, even though he's the most notorious Islamic terrorist within the western world. Osama Bin Laden is glorified throughout the Islamic world much more than George Washington is glorified in the United States.

When I was a kid, I never knew why the Islamic imams and preachers used to call Bin Laden a hero, as they claimed that he is the most authentic Muslim of their time. I never understood his actions or his mentality. I used to think of him that he's a rich Saudi who lost his mind and went on a power trip and then decided to go to war with America. I used to think that he envied America's flourished society and I really thought that he was jealous of the Jews who live in what the Arabs call Palestine. Throughout the Islamic world, I saw lots of love and support for Bin Laden and his cause, but never understood why. It turned out that he was one of the revivers of jihad, that the devout Muslims and Islamists were waiting for to come and lead them toward a certain goal; the Islamic liberation. It turned out that he was a reviver of the Islamic rebellion which is occurring; even at this very moment.

The Islamists' actions throughout the world became understandable to me once 'ISIS' declared itself as an Islamic caliphate following the Muhammadan Islamic doctrine. Before that occurred, I never understood why the Islamists and jihadists were warring with America. I also thought that they're angry at America for supporting Israel. That's one of the reasons but not the main one. It turned out that they actually want to establish an Islamic caliphate; even if physical force is needed. One of their main obstacles is the Arab governments that are blocking their way along with Israel which is located right in the middle of the

Islamic world. Today, they're taking advantage of the turbulent situations in the Middle East to encourage other Muslims to follow them and go on and engage in the jihadi project as well.

The day that I learned what the Islamic State Caliphate was up to, it confirmed to me that there is an Islamic rebellion that is taking place right under our nose. Then, I understood their actions and intentions. I was able to comprehend their situation and the reasons behind their jihadism. So basically the 9/11 attacks were meant to strike America in a manner that will change the world forever. They want to drag the western world into a religious war that will eventually cost trillions of dollars and will become a sign of power for them to present to the rest of the Muslims; that they are capable of defeating America and then replace it with an Islamic empire. So mainly, their jihadism is supposed to allow them to achieve an Islamic liberation and rebuild a Quranic caliphate. And in order for them to do so, they initiated the Islamic rebellion, which was activated by Osama Bin Laden in 1988 by the help of his fellow jihadists, by forming the Al-Qaeda Islamic jihadi organization.

Some may feel that my book spread xenophobia, but that is not accurately true. The Islamic rebellion actually is what's terrifying the world. Violent and harmful events such as the 9/11 attacks, the Boston marathon bombing and the Paris massacres is what spread xenophobia due to the religious affiliation of the attackers. The Islamic rebels, jihadists and terrorists actions' are what spread terror and fear. I simply provided a deep explanation about their personal conditions, strange actions and over-all intentions. The Islamic rebellion is an ugly reality of our time and I had provided a warning about its consequences. I really wanted to share what I know and allow the rest of my fellow Americans to share some of the knowledge that I have acquired after noticing the Islamic rebellions' results. The Islamic rebellion has been revived and is on the move. That's what I learned and became aware of after seeing the bigger picture of the radical Muslims, Islamists and jihadists during our time and era. I hope this information would allow you, the reader, to gain a deeper understanding about what's taking place, and I hope this knowledge will help us resolve with the troubling situation that we're facing today within our world. Please, check out the other 6 letters of the *warning* once they're released, they also will be very informative.